Plautus: *Trinummus*

BLOOMSBURY ANCIENT COMEDY COMPANIONS

Series editors: C. W. Marshall & Niall W. Slater

The Bloomsbury Ancient Comedy Companions present accessible introductions to the surviving comedies from Greece and Rome. Each volume provides an overview of the play's themes and situates it in its historical and literary contexts, recognizing that each play was intended in the first instance for performance. Volumes will be helpful for students and scholars, providing an overview of previous scholarship and offering new interpretations of ancient comedy.

Aristophanes: Frogs, C. W. Marshall
Aristophanes: Lysistrata, James Robson
Aristophanes: Peace, Ian C. Storey
Menander: Epitrepontes, Alan H. Sommerstein
Menander: Samia, Matthew Wright
Plautus: Casina, David Christenson
Plautus: Curculio, T. H. M. Gellar-Goad
Plautus: Menaechmi, V. Sophie Klein
Plautus: Mostellaria, George Fredric Franko
Terence: Andria, Sander M. Goldberg

Plautus: *Trinummus*

Seth A. Jeppesen

BLOOMSBURY ACADEMIC
LONDON • NEW YORK • OXFORD • NEW DELHI • SYDNEY

BLOOMSBURY ACADEMIC
Bloomsbury Publishing Plc
50 Bedford Square, London, WC1B 3DP, UK
1385 Broadway, New York, NY 10018, USA
29 Earlsfort Terrace, Dublin 2, Ireland

BLOOMSBURY, BLOOMSBURY ACADEMIC and the Diana logo are trademarks of Bloomsbury Publishing Plc

First published in Great Britain 2023

Copyright © Seth A. Jeppesen, 2023

Seth A. Jeppesen has asserted his right under the Copyright, Designs and Patents Act, 1988, to be identified as Author of this work.

Cover design: Terry Woodley
Cover image: *Forgotten Man* (detail) by Maynard Dixon, 1934.
© Brigham Young University Museum of Art

All rights reserved. No part of this publication may be reproduced or transmitted in any form or by any means, electronic or mechanical, including photocopying, recording, or any information storage or retrieval system, without prior permission in writing from the publishers.

Bloomsbury Publishing Plc does not have any control over, or responsibility for, any third-party websites referred to or in this book. All internet addresses given in this book were correct at the time of going to press. The author and publisher regret any inconvenience caused if addresses have changed or sites have ceased to exist, but can accept no responsibility for any such changes.

A catalogue record for this book is available from the British Library.

Library of Congress Cataloging-in-Publication Data
Names: Jeppesen, Seth A., author.
Title: Plautus : Trinummus / Seth A. Jeppesen.
Other titles: Bloomsbury ancient comedy companions.
Description: London : Bloomsbury Academic, 2023. | Series: Bloomsbury ancient comedy companions | Includes bibliographical references and index.
Identifiers: LCCN 2022030732 | ISBN 9781350126763 (hardback) | ISBN 9781350126770 (paperback) | ISBN 9781350126787 (epub) | ISBN 9781350126794 (ebook) | ISBN 9781350126800
Subjects: LCSH: Plautus, Titus Maccius. Trinummus. | Latin drama (Comedy–History and criticism.
Classification: LCC PA6568.T6 J47 2023 | DDC 872/.01–dc23/eng/20220826
LC record available at https://lccn.loc.gov/2022030732

ISBN: HB: 978-1-3501-2676-3
       PB: 978-1-3501-2677-0
       ePDF: 978-1-3501-2679-4
       eBook: 978-1-3501-2678-7

Series: Bloomsbury Ancient Comedy Companions

Typeset by RefineCatch Limited, Bungay, Suffolk

To find out more about our authors and books visit www.bloomsbury.com and sign up for our newsletters.

For Mark and Dorota,
mentors who opened new vistas.

Contents

List of Illustrations	viii
Preface	x
1 Introduction	1
2 Playing against Type: *Trinummus* as Roman Comedy Remix	19
3 What's Roman about *Trinummus*?	53
4 Religion in *Trinummus*	79
5 A Moral Play or a Play on Morals?	99
Conclusion	129
Appendix A: Music in *Trinummus*	131
Appendix B: A Textual Note on Line 831	135
Appendix C: Moral Sententiae in *Trinummus*	137
Notes	143
Bibliography	159
Index	167

Illustrations

Tables

2.1	Character types in *Trinummus*	25
2.2	Typical comic plot and characters	27
2.3	Transformed characters and plot in *Trinummus*	28
2.4	Potential actor–role divisions in *Trinummus*	50

Figures

2.1	The characters of *Trinummus*. *The Illustrated Sporting and Dramatic News*, Dec. 22, 1883	29
2.2	Charmides and the conman. *Black & White*, Dec. 19, 1903	44
3.1	The return of Charmides. *The Graphic*, Dec. 19, 1903	75
5.1	Painting of a performance at Westminster School. F. Fenton, 1897	102
5.2	Lesbonicus as a cricketer from the 1897 epilogue. *The Illustrated Sporting and Dramatic News*, Jan. 1, 1898	103
5.3	Rats escaping from the inn run by Lesbonicus and Stasimus; Charmides returning from the Klondyke, and the Sycophant dressed as a Turk, from the 1897 epilogue. *The Illustrated Sporting and Dramatic News*, Jan. 1, 1898	104
5.4	Lysiteles argues with Lesbonicus while Stasimus watches. *Illustrated London News*, Dec. 25, 1869	106
5.5	Characters showing class divides in the 1903 epilogue. *The Graphic*, Dec. 19, 1903	110
5.6	Men and women in the audience sitting separately at the 1869 production, with the prologue speaker depicted between the two groups. *The Graphic*, Dec. 25, 1869	111

5.7 Lady's Ticket with wax seal and handwritten date and time for the 1874 production 112
5.8 Inopia addresses the unemployed in the 1893 epilogue. *The Graphic*, Dec. 23, 1893 113

Preface

I first read *Trinummus* in graduate school, while preparing for an author-genre exam on Plautus. Given the comments I had read about the play from various scholars, I was prepared to be unimpressed. Instead, I was intrigued by a prologue speaker who refused to give the plot away and then charmed by the playful dialogue between the old men at the outset. By the time I got through the first scene, I remember thinking to myself, "This play can't be that bad: it's got buried treasure in it!" About ten years later, when Toph Marshall asked me which play I would like to write about for this series, my mind immediately went to *Trinummus*—a natural choice for a kid who always got picked last in gym class. Someone has to root for the underdogs!

Writing projects always encounter various delays and obstacles along the way, but I've never come up against one quite as daunting as the Covid-19 pandemic. I owe immense gratitude to Toph Marshall and Niall Slater, not only for their thoughtful guidance throughout this project, but for their patience as I managed a series of unforeseen delays. The same thanks go to Lily Mac Mahon, Alice Wright, and all the staff at Bloomsbury whose assistance and patience were indispensable. As is the case with all research projects, I have a whole network of scholars to thank for their insight and support at various stages. Fiona Macintosh and Claire Barnes graciously hosted my last-minute visit to the APGRD archive at Oxford and provided crucial background on the performance history of the play. Elizabeth Wells at Westminster School in London tracked down programs, reviews, and illustrations for multiple performances and provided helpful information about the history of the school and the tradition of the Latin performances there.

Here in Provo, Mike Pope assisted in working through thorny textual questions, and finding the right translation for any and all raunchy jokes. Chuck Oughton provided valuable insight into historical questions. My colleagues in the Classical Studies program at BYU and our long-suffering students heard and read versions of most of the chapters in the book and provided crucial feedback and support throughout the writing process. I especially want to thank the students in my senior seminar on *Trinummus* in Fall 2021 for contributing their thoughts on the play and providing ample opportunity to work out various aspects of my arguments. Chapter 3 of this book has gone through multiple iterations, first presented at the Mediterranean Studies Conference, May 2021, where it benefited from the feedback of Sue Shapiro and the other attendees of the session. I presented a revised version at CAMWS in March 2022, where I was aided by the thoughtful comments of Sharon James and other scholars of Roman comedy in attendance, too many to name. And of course, special thanks go out to Scott Miller and the College of Humanities at BYU for their generous support of my research trips and other necessities for this project.

None of this would have happened without the inspiration of Mark Damen, whose undergraduate class on ancient drama and subsequent mentorship on various projects instilled in me a passion for Roman comedy and an appreciation for the importance of performance, both ancient and modern. I also owe inestimable gratitude to Dorota Dutsch for helping me look for unheard voices in Roman drama and for guiding my entrance into the world of academic publishing. Every day I draw strength and encouragement from my partner Jenae and my amazing children, Eli, Quinn, and Norah ... who are no doubt so excited for me to stop talking about *Trinummus*!

1

Introduction

Plautus Then and Now

Plautus Now . . .

Darkness falls over the stacks of a library at some university. After confirming the call number, you turn down an aisle, select a shabby volume from the shelf, check the title against the assignment on the syllabus. "What's a Trinummus?" you think to yourself, as you check the author. "Titus Maccius Plautus—sounds like some stuffy old Roman guy."[1] You flip the book open with some bewilderment, and read:

> **Dramatis Personae**
> Megaronides – Old man
> Callicles – Old man
> Philto – Old man
> Charmides (*let me guess*) – Old man . . .

"Yeah, definitely some stuffy old Roman." You plop down in a reading nook with notepad ready—it's going to be a long night.

Plautus Then (*c.* 188 BCE) . . .

A warm September dawn unfolds over the city of Rome on day one of the biggest party of the year, the Roman Games [*ludi Romani*]. The city is bursting with energy, excitement, and people—people from all over. You pour out into the streets with everyone else, ready for the spectacle (and maybe some free food). You've been waiting a long time for this event, and that is true no matter who you are. You could be a senator serving as a city magistrate for the year, a knight [*eques*] planning to shore up some social connections, an aristocratic matron happy for a socially acceptable reason to leave the house, a foreign merchant eager to sell your wares, a sex worker … also eager to sell your wares, an everyday Gaius ready to blow off some steam, or even an enslaved person accompanying your master to the theater. Everyone has their own reasons to be there. Everyone is a part of the festival.

You make your way to the edges of the crowded street just as the procession begins to pass by—part parade, part religious ritual. Military recruits, athletes, dancers both serious and comical, all strut by, followed by throngs of musicians with attendants wafting incense and perfume as they go. Last of all come the litters bearing the images of the gods, with Jupiter Capitolinus most prominent among the rest. You follow the end of the procession into the Forum and watch while the gods are given seats of honor where they can observe all the performances dedicated to their worship over the coming days. Oxen with gilded horns and bright flapping fillets tied in their forelocks are ushered through the crowd, up toward the magistrates and priests who are waiting at the altar for the annual oaths and sacrifices. You put up with the tedium of watching the dictated prayers and messy entrail inspections because you know these public sacrifices may mean a free dinner of roast meat for you later, all at the city's expense.

Finally, the herald stands up to announce the slate of performances and contests for the coming days, with the aedile standing at his side, the one who planned the whole affair and who hopes you remember it when it is time to vote next year. There will be horse races and chariot races in the Circus Maximus, boxing and gladiator fights in the temporary arena set up nearby, not to mention the unofficial musicians, acrobats, tightrope walkers—maybe even dancing bears!—all busking for a few coins in whatever corner of the city they can find. But what you really want to hear about are the theatrical performances. After all, you can't just head downtown and buy a ticket to a show anytime you like, not in ancient Rome. Here you have to wait to see a show until festival time, like this one, or the Games of Apollo [*ludi Apollinares*], or the People's Games [*ludi plebeii*], or that festival that started a few years go for the Great

Mother Goddess [*ludi Megalenses*]. Like everything else on display, these plays are offerings to Jupiter and the rest of the gods. Technically speaking, they are sacred. They are not everyday kind of things.

You eagerly make your way through the crowds toward the temporary stage where the plays will happen. If you are lucky enough, or rich or important enough, maybe you get a seat on some temple steps or a shop balcony with a solid view. More likely, you're stuck standing in the back, jockeying for shoulder space, perhaps selling hot pastries or holding your master's bags. You sit through the serious performances, like the historical dramas (*fabulae praetextae*—hurray for empire!)[2] and the mythological tragedies (*fabulae crepidatae/tragoediae*—hurray for eye gouging!). Now, as the afternoon draws the shadows across porticos and temples of the Forum, it's finally time for the comedies to begin (*fabulae palliatae*—hurray for parody, mistaken identity, bad puns, and slapstick!).[3]

The crowd is getting a little rowdy and impatient, with all the honeyed wine and sausages consumed. Finally, a cheer breaks out from the back and ripples its way forward. Here they come, pushing through the audience on their way backstage, it's Plautus' troupe! (Thank Jupiter it's not those other guys! This aedile is definitely getting your vote for praetor at his next election!) You watch as they saunter by, basking in the hoots and hearty cheers of the crowd. Maybe there's a fist bump or two. There's a certain swagger here. Maybe one of them stops to strike a pose, the one everybody loved from last year's play—why not flex when you're the best, right?

The excitement grows as you hear them bustling about with costumes and props backstage. Who is going to be the mastermind of the plot to free the girl this time? Another one of those classic clever slaves, like Palaestrio (*Miles Gloriosus*) or Pseudolus (*Pseudolus*)? And where will they get the money from? Maybe they'll have to deceive the old man three times over, just like Chrysalus did a few years ago (*Bacchides*). Or maybe the women will run the show, like they did in *Casina*, or the slaves will take charge like in *Persa*. Whatever it is, you hope they do the running slave bit through the audience, that one is priceless! And the guy with the fat suit, is he going to be the pimp again (*Curculio*) or maybe he'll be pregnant with twins (*Amphitruo*)?

The herald (*praeco*) finally steps out to hush the crowd, the prologue speaker enters, the play begins. Script, actors, and audience all combine together to create that ephemeral creature we call performance—so immediate and engrossing in the moment, so hard to reconstitute after it is gone. Everything about this moment inflects your experience of the performance: the occasion, the place, the sights, sounds, and smells (gross!) of the city all combine to make this performance what it is, a one-of-a-kind creation. Even if you clone it tomorrow, it will never turn out exactly the same again. The characters respond to the audience, feeding off their energy, even breaking into improv here and there to squeeze one more laugh out of some old shtick. Lovelorn young men sigh and mope about, slaves spin elaborate schemes, old men get duped, and then duped again, which works since the plays are set in Greece, not Rome—a real Roman man wouldn't get hoodwinked like that, right? Enslaved actors turn the social strata on its head, playing venerable old masters and bankers, maybe with a subtle edge as they seize the opportunity to speak up and speak back, though, if you are an aristocrat you hardly notice—just the underlings at their games. But there are hungry eyes on the back row watching and listening for the messages that their "betters" can't hear. Sometimes comedy is serious, too. Here, in the self-proclaimed capital of the Mediterranean, enshrined in a city of brick and smoke and soot (no whitewashed marble yet, Augustus), surrounded by a panoply of voices and cultures, flanked by garishly painted statues, you watch the play unfold, full of carnivalesque inversion, bilingual jokes, and maybe even a pious prayer in Punic, the language of your bitter enemy (*Poenulus*). Rome and Greece are overlayed in a colorful pastiche, all projected through a funhouse mirror.

This is Roman comedy.

About Plautus

This image of Plautus and his troupe of actors at the festival is equal parts factual representation of a Roman festival, informed speculation, and me letting my imagination run free (only a little bit—mostly just the part about the fist-bumping). The fact of the matter is, we don't ultimately know that much about Plautus' life. Sure, there were ancient biographies of Plautus, but these were written decades, even centuries after his death and, like most ancient biographies, they relied for their details on speculations made from Plautus' own writings rather than on what we would call historical or biographical research. Despite this obstacle, there are some things that we can say with relative certainty: Plautus was born around 250 BCE and died in 184 BCE—we get the date of his death from Cicero, who tells us Plautus died in his old age, hence the guess at 250 for his birth (*Brutus* 15, *de Senectute* 14). He was originally from the town of Sarsina, in the region of Umbria, to the northeast of Rome. This means Plautus would have had a local language and identity in addition to his Roman identity and his mastery of Latin and Greek. Unlike in Athens, where actors and other theater professionals were citizens, sometimes of high standing, actors at Rome were non-citizens or were from the lower social classes, often from among the enslaved. Working as an actor prevented one from serving in the military, which was a mark of disgrace for the Romans, not of privilege, and acting could include the forfeiture of some citizen rights, including voting (a status called *infamia*).[4] One ancient biography even says that Plautus had to work in a mill like a slave in order to pay off debts incurred through failed business ventures and that he finally escaped this life through his success as a playwright (Aul. Gell. 3.3.14). While this story has long been discounted as fictional, the view it paints of the hard-scrabble life of a theater practitioner in the mid-Republic is likely accurate in tone, if not in detail.[5] In light of this, it is more likely that Plautus gained his familiarity with Greek through his association with enslaved Greek speakers on the stage and elsewhere, rather than learning it as an aristocrat with literary pretensions.

Whatever his path to the theater might have been, Plautus was certainly a success once he got there. More than one hundred titles have been attributed to Plautus, but only twenty-one plays have survived, and two of those, *Cistellaria* and *Vidularia*, are quite fragmentary. The surviving plays were the ones collected and deemed authentic by the Roman scholar Varro, some 150 years after Plautus' heyday. This appears to have been the first collection of Plautine drama as texts; previously, the plays likely only existed as working scripts and outlines used by the various acting troupes that toured Rome and the surrounding areas.[6] This detail points us to an intriguing aspect of Plautus' work as a playwright: he almost certainly did not write his plays the way we think of a playwright working today. A likely scenario is that Plautus was a leader of a troupe of actors who performed plays that consisted of portions that were written before the performance, such as the songs, and other parts that were based on improv and experimentation, crafted by the group through the processes of rehearsal and performance, not written by one playwright, a lone genius toiling away at a writing desk by himself. The scripts that Varro found likely consisted of a handful of prewritten song lyrics and scenes combined with transcripts of successful performances written down after the fact, all of which Varro then collated and compiled. This view is supported by the frequent doublets or performance variants in the plays—sets of lines that provide readers with the same information or the same joke twice, just with slightly different wording. In performance, actors would only choose one option rather than run them all back to back. The performances were likely flexible, with jokes and routines that could be extended though improv when the audience was responding well.[7] When Varro made his collection of the plays, some of the scripts had more detail and more performance variants, like *Poenulus* (1,422 lines) which includes three different endings, while others were leaner with fewer comic routines written out in full, such as *Curculio* (729 lines). When evaluating the texts of Plautus, it can be helpful to keep in mind how these plays were created, collected, and preserved.

We also know, just based on the dates of his lifetime, that Plautus lived through some extraordinary events that certainly inflected his work on the stage. Primary among these is the Second Punic War (218–201 BCE), which included Hannibal's lengthy invasion of Italy, the devastating Roman defeats at Lake Trasimene and Cannae, the ravaging of southern Italy by the Carthaginian army, and the ultimate defeat of Hannibal at the hands of Scipio Africanus at Zama. During the latter part of Plautus' life, once the Carthaginian threat was quelled, the Romans began expanding into Greece and Asia Minor, which led to an influx of wealth and new slaves, but also required many middle-class Roman citizens to be away from their homes and farms for long periods of time while on campaign in the citizen army, with no guarantee that their interests would be cared for at home. Constant warfare at home and abroad paired with privation followed by sudden prosperity surely had their effects on Plautus and his audience.

One might expect some of these issues to come up very blatantly in comedies written during this period, but direct reference to current events was hindered by the generic expectations of Roman comedy. The Romans referred to the genre that Plautus worked in as *fabulae palliatae*, which means plays in Greek dress. This name is derived from an article of Greek clothing called a *pallium*, which was a type of mantle worn over a tunic, something that set Greeks apart from the toga-wearing Romans. These plays were set in Greece and were actually adapted from Greek comedies that were written some hundred years earlier by the likes of Menander and Philemon (for more on this, see Chapter 3). The fact that these plays are nominally set in Greece at an indeterminate time means that characters don't directly discuss current events in Rome. However, for the scholar willing to dig into the details, there are many subtle references that give us insight into Roman society during the late 200s and early 100s BCE.[8]

Plautus is the oldest author in the Roman canon with complete texts that have survived, though he was part of a playwrighting tradition that stretched back to at least 240 BCE when Livius Andronicus is said to have translated the first Greek plays into Latin for performance at the *ludi Romani*, though Livius himself may well have been part of an older performance and translation tradition outside of Rome. This aspect of Plautus being the oldest surviving author yet not the original pioneer of the genre himself illustrates the odd complexities of dealing with a fragmentary literary tradition. Plautus' texts are like isolated islands floating in a sea of fragments before reaching the mainland of Caesar, Cicero, and the late Republic. To complicate matters further, the genre of the *palliatae* is one that is based on engaging with, adapting, and parodying other performances and works of literature. This includes the Greek plays on which Plautus based his adaptations (none of which Greek plays have survived in full), but also other theatrical, political, and religious performances at Rome, all of which are attested only in fragmentary form for the time of Plautus. In the absence of other contemporary texts, attempting to reconstruct the original social and literary context of Plautus can sometimes feel like watching the director's commentary without actually seeing the film itself. While this can be frustrating, it also creates a fun challenge for scholars of Roman comedy who are invested in illuminating the social, political, and historical context of our earliest Roman author.

About *Trinummus*—Haters Gonna Hate

To put it bluntly, Plautus' *Trinummus* has not been a fan favorite in recent years. The renowned classicist Ulrich von Wilamowitz-Moellendorf declared: "The *Trinummus* is boring, even for a Plautine play," and he goes on to explain how reading *Trinummus* in high school quite nearly spoiled Roman comedy for him for good.[9] Erich Segal argues: "The *Trinummus* is unique in the Plautine canon. For though Plautus wrote both good plays and bad, this is his only boring one." Alison Sharrock sums up the current scholarly consensus in the title of her 2014 chapter, "Reading Plautus' *Trinummus*: Who'd Bother?"[10] But wait—don't close this book yet! Everyone likes an underdog story and part of my reason for writing this book is to illustrate how *Trinummus* has gained this drab reputation quite undeservedly. There are a lot of genuinely funny moments in this play, but besides that, Plautus also uses *Trinummus* to make some insightful points about the society in which he lived, so stay tuned! It's going to be interesting, despite what the haters say.

If you haven't read the play yet, here's the plot: the old man Charmides is forced to go abroad to Asia, leaving his profligate son Lesbonicus and a daughter, who is unfortunately unnamed in the text, at home (lines 108–14). He also leaves a treasure of 3,000 Philippic coins hidden in the walls of the house. Charmides enjoins his neighbor Callicles to watch over his children and the treasure while he is gone. Under no circumstances is Lesbonicus to find out about the treasure, to keep him from wasting it on the proverbial riotous living. Should a marriage opportunity arise for the daughter, the treasure will serve as her dowry (149–59). All goes well until Callicles leaves town for a few days, during which time Lesbonicus promptly puts his father's house up for sale, to fund said riotous living. Callicles rushes home and pays cash for the house in order to maintain control of the treasure (165–86). When the play begins, Lesbonicus and his servant Stasimus are living in a shack on the corner of their former property (193–4) and the neighbor Megaronides, who knows nothing of the treasure, suspects that Callicles has unscrupulously taken advantage of Charmides' absence and has put the family out of their home (128–39). In the meantime, another young man, Lysiteles, seeks his father Philto's permission to marry Lesbonicus' sister without a dowry, since he has learned of the recently indigent circumstances of Lesbonicus' household (324–91). When approached by Philto and later Lysiteles about the marriage, Lesbonicus refuses to allow his sister to marry in this way and attempts to give away the family farm as a dowry, the last real asset the family possesses (435–515; 626–716). When Callicles and Megaronides find out about the marriage proposal and Lesbonicus' disastrous plans for the farm, the old men decide to dig up the treasure and hire a con artist to pretend to bring it as a dowry from the girl's father Charmides (729–819). All goes to plan, until Charmides actually arrives home and intercepts the con artist who is pretending to be a messenger from him (820–997). After a scene of comic miscommunication, Charmides finds out about the marriage and the dowry and is able to sort everything out (998–1189). The household is reunited. The family property has been preserved by watchful friends, and the young men marry their respective brides and begin their own citizen households. There's the plot—now go read the play!

*   *   *

All set? Good!

Now, you might be thinking to yourself, "A play about buried treasure can't be that boring, right?" And I agree with you. One of the reasons readers and viewers struggle with *Trinummus* nowadays is that one must have a sound understanding of the expectations of Roman comedy to really appreciate what is clever about the play. Throughout this book, I will provide readers with the extra helping of background information necessary to get as close as we can to understanding *Trinummus* as an ancient Roman would while also looking at why *Trinummus* and Roman comedy in general are still interesting today. Each chapter will consist of a brief introduction to some important aspect of Roman comedy, followed by analysis of passages from the play that elucidate the idea under consideration.

Additionally, since *Trinummus* has been a target for criticism over the past few decades, each chapter will respond to a question or complaint that readers typically have when encountering *Trinummus*. For example: Complaint 1: "I came to see the clever slave spin some outrageous grift and swindle the money to save the girl, but instead there are all these old guys on the stage." A fair objection, to be certain, and one which we will explore in Chapter 2. Roman comedy is full of stock characters and standard scenarios, but, as often happens with literature, patterns become most interesting when they are broken. Such is the case with *Trinummus*, which in many ways is like that episode of your favorite sitcom in which all the characters play against type, swapping roles and behaviors. This can be very funny, but it only works if you already know how the characters usually behave and can measure the difference. In *Trinummus*, the young man Lesbonicus becomes the blocking character, the one who hinders the marriage and who must be deceived by the comic hijinks, while the old men take on the role of *architecti doli*, the engineers of the deception. This displacement leaves

Stasimus the slave, the character type usually tasked with orchestrating the flimflam, with nothing more interesting to do than prevaricate about the quality of the family farm, and it also leaves the con artist, the usually deft henchman of the *architectus*, stuttering to even remember the name of the man from whom he is supposedly bringing the all-important letter of deception. The genius in these transpositions can only really be appreciated when considered against the backdrop of the standard plot arcs and typical characters of the *palliatae*, knowledge which Plautus' audience had but which readers today typically lack. Accordingly, this chapter will begin with a survey of the typical characters and plots of Roman comedy before diving into an analysis of how the various characters shift and play against type throughout the play.

Complaint 2: "So, Plautus just ripped off his plays from dead Greek guys and we don't even get to read the original, just the Roman, made-for-TV/direct-to-streaming spinoff?" It seems that way, but we have to remember that adaptations, as Linda Hutcheon explains, can be important works of art in their own right and we needn't discount them prima facie as being derivative.[11] Nevertheless, derivative, or even parasitic, was exactly how classicists of the eighteenth and nineteenth centuries viewed Plautine drama, as they studied it primarily as a means of reconstructing lost Greek plays. Things have fortunately changed over the last century, beginning with Eduard Fraenkel's 1922 study *Plautine Elements in Plautus* (*Plautinisches im Plautus*), but while scholars are more willing to examine Plautine comedy in its Roman context, the shadow of the elusive Greek originals still looms over much scholarship and can prevent us from really looking at what these plays would have meant in a Roman context. In Chapter 3 we will examine the relationship between the *palliatae* and the Greek originals generally, followed by an analysis of class discourse in the play. When put in the context of Roman military expansion to the east in the 190s and 180s BCE, the family of Charmides and Lesbonicus clearly represents the plight of the middle-class Roman family, likely plebeian, with the father called up to go abroad in the citizen army and the son left at home to try to guard the family interests against unscrupulous, land-hoarding elites. To Lesbonicus, Stasimus, and Charmides, it appears that they are living the nightmare scenario. The father is absent, the family wealth is gone, the neighbors have wheedled possession of the house away from the family, and the son must now choose to marry his sister off without a dowry or give away the last real property that the family owns, the farm in the country, to someone who will probably just add it to their sprawling plantation (*latifundia*). Since this is a comedy, however, these fears prove false. The neighbor who bought the house was just protecting it all along, and let's not forget about the buried treasure! Regardless of what Philemon's original Greek play might have looked like, Plautus' *Trinummus* engages the Roman audience in the social anxieties of his day and offers a temporary comic salve to assuage their fears—if only they could all go home and find fathers returned, safe and sound, and 3,000 gold coins hidden within their walls!

Complaint 3: "Plays performed at religious festivals? Thanks, but that's a hard pass on ancient pagan proselytizing." First of all, don't underestimate the fun you can have with pagans. Second, while all of Plautus' comedies were performed at religious events of some sort (festivals, temple dedications, etc.), this does not mean that they necessarily had some sort of religious message encoded in them, in the way we would think of a religious play. In Chapter 4, we will delve into the festival context of all Roman theatrical performances and examine how this religious frame would have inflected certain moments in *Trinummus*. Plautus frequently engages in religious parody that is based on the language and performance of religious rituals at Rome. Besides adding unexpected jokes to traditional prayer formulas and the like, Plautus also downgrades these pseudo-religious performances by focalizing them through slaves, sex workers, and other low-status characters, in contrast to the priests and magistrates whom the Roman audience would see performing these rituals during the festival. In *Trinummus*, the religious parodies take on an air of class discourse, which bolsters the themes of the previous chapter and draws attention to some of the presumptions of the Roman elite and their religious justifications for their social prerogatives.

Complaint 4: "This is supposed to be a comedy but instead it is just a litany of self-righteous moral maxims that come fast and thick, even from the young lover and the clever slave." Sure, no one wants the fly of moral pontification to land in their comic stew, unless, of course, there is parody involved, which is the case with *Trinummus*. In Chapter 5 we will examine how the moralizing tone of *Trinummus* has caused the play to ebb and flow in popular esteem, with the highwater mark in the 1800s, when the play was popular at posh British boarding schools. At some points, the moralizing is turned up so loud that it can't help but be funny, like when Philto and Lysiteles, father and son, do a scene that reads like it was cobbled together from a stack of motivational calendars. This is especially true when the phrases and diction of the conversation likely reflected the stern speeches of Cato and other notorious senate conservatives. When taken as independent soundbites, the torrent of moral maxims in the play can begin to sound tedious and officious (or marvelously heartwarming and socially corrective, depending on your personal threshold for schmaltzy moral droning), but I think Plautus wants it this way. Context and focalization are again important here as is class discourse. The most heavy-handed moralizing in the play is undercut by characters who either trust in gossip at the expense of facts or who are ultimately motivated by greed. To ensure that the audience doesn't miss the parody, the final and most impressive moral diatribe is focalized through the character of a drunken slave who has returned late after being bamboozled by a pack of his low-life associates, hardly the messenger of pure moral wisdom distilled from Parnassus that some want to find in the play.

Complaint 5: "Ancient literature is so boring. Am I really supposed to laugh at some dusty old play?" The answer, of course, is a resounding yes! After all of the analysis, it is important to remember that this play is a comedy, after all, and whatever serious cultural work a comedy may do, its primary job is to make the audience laugh. Repetition, wordplay, physical humor, metatheater, and the subversion of audience expectations are all tried and true methods for producing a laugh, for ancient and modern audiences alike. In *Trinummus*, Plautus serves up a variety of these comic techniques, including a number of inventive new word creations, repetition and comic echoes, a door-knocking scene with a surprise twist, followed by a classic scene of characters talking at cross purposes. Some of these moments could even have been expanded in performance as elastic gags if the audience were responding well. Opportunities for metatheatrical humor are also available through role doubling by the actors. When considered as performance and within the generic expectations of Roman comedy, there are a lot of genuinely funny moments in *Trinummus*. Throughout the book, I will address these moments of humor when they are germane to the topics at hand, which means I get to be the guy at the party who goes around explaining jokes to everyone. Who doesn't love that?

That is what you can expect for the book going forward. Now, before we set off on our analysis of the play, let's talk about when *Trinummus* was first performed. One of the tricky aspects of studying Plautine comedy is that the manuscripts include dates for only two of the plays (*Stichus*, 200 BCE; *Pseudolus*, 191 BCE). For the rest, scholars try to find references to known events in Roman history to establish a window during which the text must have been written—the *terminus post quem* is the earliest time a piece could have been written and the *terminus ante quem* is the latest time a piece could have been written. At *Trin.* 990, the conman tells Charmides that he will make sure the new aediles give him a beating. Roman magistrates assumed their new offices in the spring which means that the aediles could only truly be thought of as new at the *ludi Megalenses*, the games for the Great Mother Goddess performed in the first week of April.[12] This religious festival only featured theatrical events from 194 BCE on, so 194 becomes the *terminus post quem* for the play. Further information about the date can be gleaned from line 872, in which the con artist refers to a recent census. The best candidates for this are the censuses of 194 and 189 BCE Niall Slater prefers the earlier census and dates the play to 192 BCE while Wolfgang de Melo, relying on references to Syrian slaves supposedly coming from the war against Antiochus III (192–188 BCE), places the date of the play in 188 or 187 BCE[13] Either of these options places

Trinummus toward the end of Plautus' career and firmly within the period of Roman expansion toward the east.

Why Read Plautus Today?

Establishing this context is important because it helps us see what *Trinummus* could have meant to its original Roman audience. Despite its detractors, *Trinummus* is actually the perfect play for exploring the complexities of Plautine dramaturgy and the potential social impact of Roman comedy during the mid-Republic. During Plautus' day, Rome was still a republic, but in the realm of foreign relations it was a de facto territorial empire. Having consolidated control of Italy and Sicily, Rome was rapidly expanding into Spain in the west and Greece and Asia Minor in the east. Frequently, these wars were not, on the surface, wars of territorial expansion—there were alliances to protect, red lines that couldn't be crossed without response. But, whatever the justification, wars, as they always do, made the rich richer and the poor, well ... dead. The period after the threat of Hannibal in the Second Punic War should have been a time of relief and prosperity for Romans at home, and for some it certainly was. Vast fortunes could be had through success on the battlefield and the plunder that Roman generals so freely claimed, not to mention the eventual tax revenues from future provinces. Unfortunately, this wealth did not trickle down to those who would have benefited the most from it (as history teaches us, of the many things that trickle down in a teeming metropolis, wealth is not one of them). The second century BCE was a disastrous time for the Roman middle class, who bore the brunt of an endless demand for citizen soldiers while spiraling further and further into debt.

In some ways, it is fortunate that the contemporary voice that we have from this period is not that of a self-assured elite historian or politician but that of a low-status busker of popular comedies who can provide us with the view from below. As Amy Richlin has pointed out in her book *Slave Theater in the Roman Republic*, the *palliatae* were plays crafted and performed by slaves and freedmen, and the view they provide us of everyday folk shows us people shackled by debt, hunger, and physical suffering. The voice of Plautus is, on one hand, a voice of laughter and comic exuberance, but if you peel back the veneer of the topsy-turvy carnivalesque, it is also a voice of parody and critique, a voice that speaks of how life could be different if we could find a way to live in the comic now, and not return to the everyday life of the forum, the mill, and the plantation. The plays are full of what James C. Scott calls hidden transcripts, messages that the subjugated in any culture share with each other, out of sight of those in control.[14] The funny thing about hidden transcripts, though, is that they are not really hidden at all. In the case of Plautus, they are performed right under the noses of the elite, who, if they cared to pay attention, might easily notice. It is valuable to have voices that question the grand narratives of Roman history, even if we have to extricate those voices from the web of comic discourse into which they have been woven.

In reading this description of Rome during the mid-Republic, some things probably sound uncomfortably familiar. We live in a moment in which people in the US and around the world are becoming in equal parts more critical and more invested in the grand narratives of the elites, whether those narratives are about race relations, national origins and destinies, or even the efficacy of modern democracy. Social media is amplifying both sides of the debate—it allows marginalized voices to come to the fore, but it also has the capacity to amplify deceptive narratives that keep us tied to the same old oppressive ideologies. Plautus' Rome witnessed the birth of the imperial ideologies that eventually morphed into European colonialism. Beginning with the final, desperate words of Eric Garner and spreading to Black Lives Matter protests across the globe, cries of "We can't breathe!" remind us that, in so many ways, we are still struggling to catch our breath amidst the smoking embers of empire. But despite the ostensibly postcolonial phase we have entered, the same players are still making the same moves on the chessboard, but now under the guise of economic neo-imperialism, which turns out to be just as effective in its coercion as its less subtle older sibling.

When white supremacists boldly claim, even while storming the US capitol, that they are the rightful heirs of an imagined Greco-Roman white utopia, we need the voices from below to shatter that illusion and shine the light of parody and critique on this supposed birthright of a superior Western civilization with a divine destiny. We need a glimpse of Rome from below, as real Romans saw it, not the fly-over, CGI drone footage of pristine columns and gleaming statues. We need to read Plautus now, and we need to see him not as a subpar Roman wholesaler of B-side Greek hits, as earlier generations of classicists have frequently seen him, but instead we need to recognize the playwright with the courage to enact onstage the hunger, pain, and desperation of his times, the playwright who can stand in the forum, mock the powerful, and smile with each twist of the knife.

On a personal note (as if the foregoing wasn't personal), I proposed this book in 2018 and began drafting it in 2019. Then Covid hit, derailing travel, research, and writing plans for this project, but, more significantly, sifting over our entire existence a thin, cold dust of loss, isolation, divisiveness, and pain. Comedy comes from a place of pain and distress. What need would we have for laughter if everything were smooth and pleasant? Plautus and his actors understood pain. They understood hunger. They understood the desperation of struggling against a rigged system of predetermined winners and losers. When times are hard, we often say we need a good laugh, but I believe that in times like these, our need for comic relief does not lie solely in a desire for escapism. Rather, we laugh because in laughing together, even across millennia, we are sharing a moment of human understanding with someone who feels the same way we do. Sometimes the shared feeling is joy or freedom. Sometimes it is fear, or sorrow, or just a deep, longing desperation. Whatever the source, we laugh together, through the tears—and the show goes on.

2

Playing against Type: *Trinummus* as Roman Comedy Remix

Sit down and turn on a sitcom. It could be from the 1970s or from last week, it doesn't really matter. As you watch the actors stumble through a series of miscommunications and domestic dust-ups, you'll notice some patterns in the characters who appear and the ways they behave. There will likely be a grouchy old man trying to ruin everyone's fun, a young man trying to get a girl who is way out of his league, and a glutton who, try as he might, just can't get enough food, sex, etc. Maybe there will be a schemer who hatches elaborate plans that seldom pan out, or perhaps a stern wife/girlfriend/mother whom our comic heroes must avoid in order to have their fun. And then, all of a sudden, the boss walks in and sees everything! But don't worry—no one gets sacked. They all need to be back doing what they do for next week's episode.

Comedy in the Western tradition has thrived for millennia on a remixing of recurring character types who bungle their way through a series of standard scenarios. The characters and the scenes may shift and transform over time and across cultures, but the similarities remain. Audiences apparently derive pleasure from seeing their favorite characters deliver their classic lines and perform their standard shtick. Ralph Kramden shakes his fist at Alice, "One of these days, Alice ... Bang! Zoom! You're goin' to the moon" (*The Honeymooners*), Jim does something outrageous to Dwight's stapler, again, (*The Office*), or Joey saunters up next to some too beautiful coffee house patron and says, "How you doin'?" (*Friends*). The laugh track goes wild! Every show or every subgenre has its own favorite set of running gags and repeat one-liners. The Romans, for example, couldn't get enough of people knocking on doors: Character 1 (*banging violently on the door*) "Hello, hello? Is anyone home?" Character 2 (*throwing open the door*) "Hey, what's the big idea? Does this door owe you money? You're beating it off its hinges!" Comic gold! (If you're a Roman.)[1]

But sometimes the humor works the other way around and the characters do the opposite of what we expect. This time Dwight shows up at the office dressed like Jim and turns Jim's pranks back on the prankster, or maybe an inebriated Rachel smiles and aims the "How you doin'?" pick-up line back at Joey. Of course, for humor of this sort to work, time has to be spent setting up those expectations in advance. In *Trinummus*, we get only half of this equation. Much of the humor in the play comes from characters playing against type and confounding the audience's expectations, but this humor can be easily lost if the reader or viewer is not well versed in the recurring character types and common plot motifs of Roman comedy. As Alison Sharrock explains, "*Trinummus*, at least to a modern audience, needs the help of a knowledge of other plays, in order that its games can be appreciated."[2] To that end, we will run through a quick overview of typical characters and plots in Roman comedy so that we have some models with which to compare the material from *Trinummus* and thus get an accurate picture of the games that Plautus plays with the audience's expectations. When we turn our analysis to *Trinummus*, we will see that the old men in the play stake a claim to the trickster role that is usually reserved for the clever slave, and in so doing, they leave Stasimus and the Sycophant with little to do but flail and flounder about. This displacement of the trickster role causes a series of displacements throughout the play. The role of blocking character, left open by the old men, is filled by the most improbable of characters for this responsibility, the profligate young man. Everyone ends up playing against type and the whole Plautine upside-down cake is then covered with a thick icing of ironic moralizing. In the end, the plot that the old men hatch for getting a dowry to Lesbonicus' sister fails, but this doesn't really matter, since, of all the denizens of the Plautine stage (and downtown Rome, for that matter), the old men do not need comic scheming to accomplish their purposes. Since they already possess the power and resources, they can only fail up, as the saying goes. Although the play withholds from the audience the satisfaction of seeing the scheme come to fruition, it delivers in a different way: *Trinummus* gives viewers the pleasure of seeing their favorite characters trying their hand at impersonating each other, which is hilarious in its own right.

~~Stock~~ Characters and ~~Standard~~ Plots

Studying typical character types can be useful for understanding the dynamics of Roman comedy, but there are also some dangers involved with this approach. A criticism frequently leveled at Roman comedy is that "if you've read one play, you've read them all," implying that the plots and characters are practically interchangeable; however, a thoughtful examination of the Plautine corpus proves such an assertion false. The benefit of exploring stock characters and standard plots is that it gives the reader/viewer the ability to discern patterns within the genre. The danger, however, comes when one substitutes pattern recognition for interpretation. If all you do as a reader is pin the name tag "clever slave" on Chrysalus (*Bacchides*) or Palaestrio (*Miles Gloriosus*) or Tranio (*Mostellaria*), you run the risk of homogenizing a vibrant set of individual characters under a label that seeks to limit what a character can do or represent in a play, not to mention the fact that each of these characters would, I think, resent the simplification. (I would, however, like to be present in the room where the name tags are handed out, just to see what happens!) Recognizing stock characters and plots within a play can be a good starting point for interpretation, but to really get at the heart of a given play, one must delve into what makes the characters and the plot unique. In this sense, the variations from the pattern, not the pattern itself, end up being more meaningful in the long run, but to get to that point, you must learn the pattern first.

At the outset of this examination, it is helpful to point out that the character types we refer to as stock characters are not just modern formulations that we project onto the ancient material. The Romans themselves used these categories when talking about their own theatrical traditions.³ For example, while Ovid waxes poetic about the immortality offered through literary fame, he claims that Menander will live on as long the deceitful slave (*fallax servus*), harsh father (*durus pater*), dishonest bawd (*improba lena*), and flattering sex worker (*meretrix blanda*) still roam the stage (*Amores* 1.15.17–18).⁴ Terence, when responding to complaints that he stole characters from other plays, provides a list of stock characters that frequently appear in Greek and Roman comedies, including the running slave (*currentem servom*), honest matrons (*bonas matronas*), clever sex workers (*meretrices malas*), the braggart soldier (*gloriosum militem*), and the greedy parasite (*parasitum edacem*), the kind that is an ever-munching sidekick of soldiers and well-off young men, not the type one gets from poorly cooked sausage. Plautus himself refers to some of these categories in the prologue of *Captivi* (The Captives) by way of explaining what viewers will not see in this particular play, including the aforementioned clever sex worker and braggart soldier, but adding to the list a mendacious pimp (*peiiurus leno*, 57–8). Not only does Plautus comment on the common labels for these characters, but he also makes jokes about the typical situations they find themselves in, as when the young lover Calidorus metatheatrically explains to his slave Pseudolus that plays are no fun, "unless the lover acts like an idiot" (*Pseudolus* 238).

Only some of the common character types show up in *Trinummus*, so for the purposes of this play, here are the "usual suspects":

Servus callidus, aka Clever slave
   Answers to: Chrysalus (*Bacchides*), Pseudolus, Tranio (*Mostellaria*), Palaestrio (*Miles Gloriosus*), et al., sometimes Stasimus.⁵
   Description: red hair, potbelly, thick calves, sharp eyes, swollen head, with ridiculously massive feet (*Pseudolus* 1218–20). A criminal mastermind fated to serve inferior intellects, constantly writing and performing plays-within-a-play.
   Modus operandi: Swindles money for his young master through clever use of costumes, letters, signet rings, and minor cast members.

Frequently known to deceive pimps, bankers, and garrulous old men. Has been known, among other crimes, to impersonate military personnel (*Pseudolus*), fabricate twin siblings (*Miles*), swindle his master three times in the same day (*Bacchides*), hide raucous partying with campy tales of noisy poltergeists (*Mostellaria*), and celebrate minor successes with heavy drinking (*passim*).

Adulescens amans, aka Goofy young lover

Answers to: Calidorus (*Pseudolus*), Pleusicles (*Miles Gloriosus*), Phaedromus (*Curculio*), Alcesimarchus (*Cistellaria*), et al., sometimes Lesbonicus or Lysiteles.

Known associates: clever slaves, sneaky sex workers, and damsels in distress.

Description: A jaunty young gentleman, irreparably in love with a girl he can't get. Amid troubles, feckless; in danger, craven. Often given to inane prattle, bursts of song, and grandiose threats of suicide.

Modus operandi: Falls in love with a current or future sex worker, who may or may not actually be a freeborn Athenian girl. Needs copious amounts of cash to either buy her attention or purchase her freedom. Spends the play weeping, moaning, and nearly blowing their cover.

Senex durus, aka Stern old man

Answers to: Simo (*Pseudolus*), Theopropides (*Mostellaria*), Nicobolus (*Bacchides*), et al., sometimes Megaronides, Callicles, Philto, and Charmides.

Description: Cantankerous father, relative, or neighbor of the *adulescens*, determined to prevent the love affair from continuing. White hair and beard. Prone to long moralizing speeches and threats of violence.

Known associates: Dutiful slaves, bankers, tutors, gentlemen of state ... oh, and pimps, of course.

Modus operandi: Douses the fun with an inexhaustible stock of folksy anecdotes about the good old days.

Senex lepidus, aka Charming old man

Answers to: Periplectomenus (*Miles Gloriosus*), sometimes Megaronides, Callicles, and Philto.

Description: Same physical description as the *senex durus* but determined to show the kids these days that he is still "cool, daddy-o." Dedicated to helping the love plot and deception succeed. Prone to long obnoxious speeches about how much fun he is at parties.

Known associates: Young lover, clever slave, various young ladies of mild-to-ill repute.

Modus operandi: Inexplicably offers his house, servants, and wads of cash to the young lover to help the deception plot thrive. Loves to corner youngsters at the party and gas on about his social graces and impeccable geriatric hygiene.

Servus fidelis, aka Dutiful slave

Answers to: Messenio (*Menaechmi*), Grumio (*Mostellaria*), Trachalio (*Rudens*), sometimes Stasimus

Description: Same physical description as the clever slave, but with smaller feet. Frequently running and out of breath. Much less fun and much more angst than his troublemaking counterpart.

Known associates: Old men and young lovers.

Modus operandi: Hops to whenever duty calls in hopes of earning his freedom by the end of the play. Prone to long speeches about the virtue of obedience and other comic buzzkills. Sometimes does the running slave bit [*servus currens*], careening about the stage at top speed with crucially trivial information that he just has to shout to everyone he meets.

Sycophanta, aka Scheming conman

Answers to: Everything and nothing (unnamed in *Trinummus*)

Description: Grifter for hire. Ready to be anyone or anything if the price is right. Frequently the key to the deception plot, but something of a loose cannon. The bane of bankers, pimps, and overconfident old men.

Known associates: Young lovers and clever slaves.

Modus operandi: Sells his services to whichever faction pays best. A master of disguise and intrigue, though sometimes forgetful and tends to abscond with his costume.

When the audience sits down to watch *Trinummus*, these are the characters they expect to see onstage because they are the ones that they have seen before in so many other comedies. Since the audience would have experienced the play as performance and not text, it is important to remember that there were visual aspects to these stock characters as well, and the masks and costumes could say as much about a character's identity as the words they spoke. The visual aspects of the character types from *Trinummus* are summarized in Table 2.1. In general, Roman comedy employed five mask types inherited from Greek New Comedy, but frequently mixed in elements from native Italian traditions as well.[6] Three of these mask types were used for male characters: old men had white hair and beards, slaves had dark (i.e., non-white) hair and beards, and young men had dark hair with no beard.[7] Thus, these mask types could differentiate between age and social status (slave or free), but many of the details of characterization were left to the dialogue and the actors' physical choices in performance. In the case of the old men, there were likely no visual distinctions between the stern [*durus*] and pleasant [*lepidus*] types, though a mask with asymmetrical eyebrows could have been used to simulate a sudden flare of temper for the *senex durus*.[8] Similarly, there were not necessarily any visual cues to distinguish the clever slaves from the faithful ones, but such distinctions were readily apparent in the behavior of the

Table 2.1 Character types in *Trinummus*

Character name	Mask/appearance
Young man [*adulescens*]	Dark hair, no beard
Clever slave [*servus callidus*]	Dark (possibly red) hair and beard, potentially with asymmetrical eyebrows
Faithful slave [*servus fidelis*]	Dark hair and beard
Stern old man [*senex durus*]	White hair and beard, possibly with asymmetrical eyebrows
Pleasant old man [*senex lepidus*]	White hair and beard
Conman [*sycophanta*]	Dark hair and beard, fanciful costume based on the required deception (military, traveling foreigner, etc.)

characters in question.[9] In *Trinummus*, Plautus plays with this visual ambiguity by giving the audience conflicting information in the dialogue. For example, the moralizing tone that Megaronides, Callicles, and Philto all assume makes them appear like the stern old man type [*senex durus*], but their determination to help the marriage succeed aligns them more with the pleasant type [*senex lepidus*]. The interplay between behavior and appearance only heightens the sense of surprise when the characters fail to behave as expected.

From these descriptions of stock characters, it is also easy to piece together the basic building blocks of the comic plot. As the saying goes, comedies end with a wedding, which is often the case with Roman comedies as well, except for when the wedding is replaced with a contract with the young lover's call girl of choice—sometimes the love interest in question is not of the right social standing for the characters to get married, in which cases partying and sex is the ultimate goal. The typical Roman comic love plot goes something like this: young man is infatuated with a girl he can't have. Common obstacles include a lack of money, a cantankerous father (the young man's or sometimes the young woman's, as in *Aulularia*), a previous commitment to a blowhard soldier, the machinations of a scheming pimp who has cheated the young lover or otherwise just does not want to give the girl up, or maybe the woman in question has raised her prices and the young man is flat broke. The solution to this problem almost invariably features some sort of metatheatrical deception, with a subset of the characters performing a play-within-a-play for an internal audience so as to unite the lovers at the end, usually with the clever slave as the playwright and director, a role that scholars sometimes refer to as the *architectus doli* (architect of deception).[10] Once the basic conflict is set up, the characters take sides. The young men, young women, devious sex workers, clever slaves, parasites, conmen, and pleasant old men work to help the love plot succeed, while the stern old men, pimps, bankers, angry wives, soldiers, and cruel procuresses (female pimps) serve as blocking characters, who work to prevent the lovers from getting together. In the end, the blocking characters are defeated and usually acknowledge the deception that has

Table 2.2 Typical comic plot and characters

Goal: Get the young lovers together	
(* appears in *Trinummus*)	
Team 1 – Working for the young lovers	**Team 2 – Blocking characters**
Young man [*adulescens*]*	Angry old man [*senex durus*]*
Clever slave [*servus callidus*]*	Banker [*trapezita*]
Faithful slave [*servus fidelis*]*	Moneylender [*danista*]
Parasite [*parasitus*]	Braggart soldier [*miles gloriosus*]
Pleasant old man [*senex lepidus*]*	Angry wife/mother [*matrona*]
Conman [*sycophanta*]*	Pimp [*leno*]
Young marriageable woman [*virgo, pseudo-meretrix*]	Procuress [*lena*]
Sex worker [*meretrix*]	

been carried out against them. Punishment is threatened against the scheming slaves who orchestrate the madness but is never carried out—the Romans preferred to reserve such things for the return to real life after the play.[11] Table 2.2 shows how these characters fit into the typical comic love plot.

As I noted earlier, character types and generalized plot summaries are useful to an extent in setting up the audience's background knowledge and expectations, but we must be careful here not to assume that every Roman comedy followed this outline exactly. For as many as fit this pattern quite well (e.g., *Bacchides*, *Pseudolus*, *Miles Gloriosus*, *Mostellaria*) there are just as many that do not follow this scheme at all or only do so loosely (e.g., *Captivi* and *Amphitruo*). It is also worth pointing out that besides the divine prologue speakers, no female characters appear onstage in *Trinummus*, though given the plot, we might expect to see a sex worker as a love interest for Lesbonicus and perhaps briefly see his sister, though it was uncommon for unmarried, freeborn women to appear as speaking characters. While this lack of female characters (and even a lack of a name for the sister!) can be taken as just more evidence of Roman misogyny, let's not forget that the action of the play centers on a network of citizen males who are all working hard to provide a safe and successful future for this young woman, a remarkable rebuttal to the idea that daughters were only liabilities in ancient Greece and Rome.[12]

This outline of typical characters and plots from Roman comedy sets the baseline for what Plautus' audience would be expecting at the beginning of *Trinummus*. What they get instead is an elaboration of new types that cause the characters to switch teams, as it were, as shown in Table 2.3. The old men steal the role of schemers, becoming clever old men [*senes callidi*] who use comic trickery to keep their friend's money safe and arrange a marriage for his daughter. This appropriation of the trickster role sets off a series of displacements that transforms the young men into blocking characters, stern young men [*adulescentes duri*], who try to prevent the marriage and complain about the dangers of love. Even the conman ends up on the side of the blocking characters, as an obstacle that needs to be overcome by Charmides. Philto, the stern moralizer, ends up advocating for the marriage, the usual purview of

Table 2.3 Transformed characters and plot in *Trinummus*: A remix

Team 1 – *Working for the young lovers (i.e., preserve the treasure, secure a dowry, and accomplish the marriage)*	Team 2 – *Blocking characters*
Clever old men [*senes callidi*] Callicles, Megaronides, and Charmides all act as plotting tricksters.	**Stern young men [*adulescentes duri*]** Lesbonicus tries to stop the wedding; Lysiteles talks like a *senex durus*
Pleasant old man [*senex lepidus*] Philto acts as go-between to get the couple together	**Conman [*sycophanta*]** The hired conman acts as an obstacle to be overcome by Charmides
Faithful slave [*servus fidelis*]/ Clever slave [*servus callidus*] Stasimus wants the marriage to succeed but tries to block the dowry. He is eager for the return of Charmides but colludes with Lesbonicus in wasting money.	

Playing against Type: Trinummus *as Roman Comedy Remix* 29

Figure 2.1 The characters of *Trinummus*. *The Illustrated Sporting and Dramatic News*, Dec. 22, 1883. Reproduced by kind assistance of the Governing Body of Westminster School.

the pleasant old man [*senex lepidus*], while Stasimus ends up in limbo between the roles of clever slave [*servus callidus*] and faithful slave [*servus fidelis*], ultimately turning down the opportunity to elaborate a full-scale deception. Instead, the old men, Megaronides and Callicles, devise a rather vanilla scheme for the conman who ends up being defeated by the surprisingly witty Charmides when he arrives home. In all these twists and turns, it is the way the characters behave contrary to expectations that brings out the laughs in *Trinummus*.

Old Guys Rule

Immediately following the prologue, Megaronides is intent on chastising his friend Callicles for apparently cheating Lesbonicus, his ward, out of his house. Callicles reluctantly reveals the secret of the treasure to Megaronides and the two agree to work together to protect the interests of Charmides' family and to keep Lesbonicus from getting his hands on the treasure. On the surface, the scene appears to be a typical moment of exposition on the go, but upon closer examination, the old men give a number of clues to the audience about their intention to take over the role of tricksters-in-charge [*architecti doli*], clues that are easy for a modern reader to miss but which would have been apparent to Plautus' audience, steeped in the traditions of Roman theater as they were.

First of all, the overall setup of the scene, with the chummy banter between the old men, is reminiscent of other exposition scenes in Plautus that involve clever slave characters rather than old men. For example, *Persa* begins with an exchange between the two slaves Toxilus and Sagaristio, in which they discuss how Toxilus needs money to buy his girlfriend's freedom (7–53). The second act of *Asinaria* features a similar scene in which the slaves Libanus and Leonida provide the exposition for the deception scheme in their play (267–380). In each of these scenes, the enslaved characters exchange anecdotes about the various punishments they have received from their masters and joke about who has received the worst torture. The banter of the old men follows a similar pattern, but with jokes about their wives' longevity replacing jokes about masters and punishment. They even trade misogynistic jibes about swapping wives to see who gets the better deal (51–64). When compared with various slave greeting scenes in Plautus, the old men in *Trinummus* employ a similar verbal palette of suspicion, accusation, and torment, with the addition of language of disease and sickness—they are crotchety old men after all. The similarities between the exposition provided by the old men in *Trinummus* and that provided by the clever slaves in other plays signals to the audience that Callicles and Megaronides will be doing something other than their typical blocking roles in this play.

Besides the overall composition and tone of the scene, there are also a few details in the language that highlight the intention of Callicles and Megaronides to seize control of the intrigue in the play. Immediately after Callicles enters the stage, Megaronides turns to the audience and, pointing to his friend, says, "This is the guy who in his old age has become a boy" (*Hic ille est senecta aetate qui factust puer*, 43).[13] In the context of the scene, this is meant as an insult pertaining to Callicles' allegedly unsuitable behavior toward his ward, but in a metatheatrical sense, this line announces to the audience that the old men are not going to be playing according to type in this play. Furthermore, Megaronides' aside to the audience aligns him with the tricksters in comedy, whose frequent asides help them build a closer rapport with the audience than the other characters onstage.[14]

An additional similarity between the language in this scene and the language of Plautine tricksters can be found in lines 145–52, in which Callicles finally reveals the secret of the treasure to Megaronides:

Meg Whatever you trust to me, you can pick up where you left it.

Cal **Just look around** [*circumspicedum*] you and make sure there are no witnesses present with us; I ask again, **look around!** [*circumspice*]

Meg If you say something, I'm listening.

Cal If you're silent, I'll speak. When Charmides set out from here abroad, he showed me a treasure in this very house. Quick, **look around**! [*circumspice*] **MEG** No one is there!

Cal . . . a treasure of 3,000 Philippic coins.

Trinummus 140–52 (emphasis added)

On one level, the repetition of the command "look around" [*circumspice*] is a type of metatheatrical joke that Plautus is particularly fond of. Character 1 says "Look around, make sure we are alone!" Character 2 (*looking right at the audience*) "Yup, there's no one else here." Cue the rimshot and laugh track. On another level though, this language connects Callicles with other famous Plautine tricksters. In *The Haunted House*, when the clever slave Tranio is about to spin his deceptive tale about the house being haunted, he has the following exchange with his master Theopropides, who has recently returned from abroad:

Theo Speak, what is it?

Tra First **look around** [*circumspicedum*]; is there anyone who might overhear our conversation?

Theo It's very safe.

Tra **Look around** [*circumspice*] again!

Theo There is no one here! Speak now!

Mostellaria 472–4 (emphasis added)

A similar exchange occurs in *The Braggart Soldier* when the clever slave Palaestrio begins weaving his deception for the soldier Pyrgopolynices:

Pal **Look around** [*circumspicedum*], so that no one overhears our conversation, since I was ordered to handle this business in secret.

Pyrg No one is here!

Miles Gloriosus 955–7 (emphasis added)

After this exchange, Palaestrio draws his webs of deception around Pyrgopolynices with a fabricated tale about a ring that is supposedly a love token from a woman who wants to have an affair with the soldier.

Again, the phrase "look around" [*circumspice*] is used to signal the revelation of important material and the beginning of the play-within-a-play.¹⁵ When compared to these other scenes, the "look around" bit in *Trinummus* functions to further announce the intention of the old men to stake a claim to the role of *architectus doli*. One important difference between the scene in *Trinummus* and these other scenes is that in the latter the tactic is used to present false information to the gullible internal audience of the play-within-a-play, while in *Trinummus* the device is used to highlight a true detail of the backstory, one that will become important for the play-within-a-play starring the hired conman later. Could this be an early cue to the ultimate ineffectiveness of the deception that the old men eventually fabricate, or perhaps an invitation to the audience to consider carefully whether they are the ones being deceived by the appearance of the old men? Either way, the similarity in the language that the old men use and the language of Plautus' most inveterate tricksters indicates to the audience that the old men intend to control the deception plot in *Trinummus*. Putting the old men in this role upsets the balance in the comic plot and sets off a series of displacements. Moralizing old men like Megaronides and Callicles typically function as blocking characters in Plautus, but with their decision to take charge of the trickery in the play, someone else must step in and provide the conflict. If the role of clever slave can be appropriated by the old men, the least likely in the world of Plautus to run the play-within-a-play, then why not bring the young men in as blocking characters? In the world of *Trinummus*, it makes perfect sense!

Where have all the Young Men Gone?

After setting up a play with spoken exposition, Plautus loves to transition to exuberant song and dance numbers, and *Trinummus* doesn't disappoint (see Appendix A for the musical structure of *Trinummus*).¹⁶ Lysiteles comes onstage singing a vivid song in mixed meters about the difficulty inherent in deciding whether to devote one's life to the pursuit of love [*amor*] or wealth [*res*] (223–75). After a long list of the ills that one can endure when snagged in the clutches of love, a list that includes some of Plautus' most playfully invented words, like *blandiloquentulus* (little flattery-flapping git, 239) and *sandaligerulae* (sandal-carrier-ess-in-waiting, 252a), Lysiteles decides to reject the amorous life in favor of industry, an apt decision for a character whose name is derived from a Greek adjective meaning profitable.[17] Lysiteles boldly declares, "Get lost, Love, you are not pleasing and I won't use you at all! (*apage te, Amor, non places, nil te utor*, 258) and he underlines this rejection by using language from legally binding pronouncements of divorce, "Love, take your things for yourself," (*Amor, tuas res tibi habeto*, 266a).[18] Lysiteles' reasons for his decision are focused on questions of wealth and social status. He claims that lovers, through their attempts to be obliging to those they love, end up impoverished (255), an unacceptable outcome, since, as he then remarks, "when someone is poor, they are of such little worth!" (*ubi qui eget, quam preti sit parvi*, 257)—fine sentiments, I suppose, for a young aristocrat, but not in keeping with the standard behavior of young men in comedy. In fact, Lysiteles would be hard pressed to find a more forceful way to reject the role of young lover [*adulescens amans*] than what we see in the lyrics of this song.

Lysiteles underlines the rejection of this character type when his father Philto enters the stage. Rather than hiding and eavesdropping on the old man, which is standard behavior, Lysiteles instead immediately announces to Philto:

> **Lys** Father, I am here, command whatever you desire!
> I will not cause you delay, nor will I furtively
> hide myself from your gaze.
>
> 277–8a

I imagine passionate boos from the audience at this point. A young man who refuses to eavesdrop on his decrepit old father, what kind of comedy is this anyway? The forcefulness of the rejection could draw laughter, however, in the way the young man metatheatrically comments on what he sees as the shameful behavior of his *adulescentes* counterparts.

Lysiteles continues in a similar vein, announcing somewhat shockingly that he considers himself a slave to his father's commands (*tuis servivi servitutem imperiis*, 302), an extreme and likely distasteful iteration of the Roman concept of *patria potestas*, the father's ultimate authority over even adult children. As Philto pours a torrent of moral maxims down on his son's head, Lysiteles nods along in agreement, even adding, in priggish fashion:

> I have always kept these sayings of yours as a shield for my youth,
> so that I don't enter anywhere where there is a speakeasy of
>   corruption,
> or go walking about at night, or take something away from another
>   person,
> or ever cause any grief to you father, I vehemently refrain from that.
> So far, I've kept all your precepts patched and thatched by my
>   temperance.
>
> 313–17

This anthology of juvenile delinquent deeds that Lysiteles says he will never commit is basically the to-do list of every other young lover in Plautus. "Let's see, what do I have on the docket for today: go carousing at night—check; take stuff that doesn't belong to me—check; cause my father grief—check; enter a speakeasy of corruption (*damni conciliabulum*, 314)—double check!" Despite the poetic verve with which he expresses these sentiments (particularly note the jingling assonance and bouncy rhythm of line 317), in the end, Lysiteles comes off as somewhat of a buzzkill, and an inconsistent one at that, since begging your father to allow you to marry without a dowry is hardly a rejection of love in favor of financial profit.

Lysiteles does, however, make good on his commitment not to play the role of the typical comic *adulescens*. He involves his father from the beginning, he rejects eavesdropping and comic deception, he does not collude with a clever slave character, and he tries to remove the need for someone to produce a pile of money in order for the love plot to succeed—all polar opposite behaviors to those found in the typical *adulescens* playbook. While the sentiments expressed by Lysiteles do not match his young man's costume and mask, the rejection of love and fatuous moralizing do fit a familiar mold. These are the sayings of the old men in comedy who try to prevent the deception and love plot from succeeding. Just as Megaronides and Callicles signaled to the audience that they intended to take on the role of clever slave, Lysiteles in this scene announces that he will be playing the stern old man [*senex durus*] in this play.

If Lysiteles is the stern old man, then where does this leave his father Philto? Lysiteles dedicates himself to a boring, citizen marriage from the outset and insists that no money in the form of a dowry be produced for the marriage to succeed, and he does all of this while competing with Philto to see who can deliver the sappiest moral sentiment to the audience (for more on this, see Chapter 5). This unexpected behavior on Lysiteles' part compels his father into a surprising situation: Philto is forced to transform from the stern, moralizing old man [*senex durus*] to the charming old man who makes sure the love plot succeeds [*senex lepidus*], in this case still with a heavy dose of moralizing. When Philto enters, he gives every indication that he will be a blocking character in the play, with gems like these: "He alone is honorable, who is dissatisfied with how honorable he is" and "He who constantly condemns himself is the one with a true talent for diligence" (320, 322). But suddenly Philto finds himself agreeing to arrange his son's marriage, a situation he describes in this way: "Well these things aren't the best, nor as I deem fair, but they're better than the worst" (392–3). These lines certainly refer to Philto's opinion on being coerced into arranging his son's marriage with a dowerless bride, but on a metatheatrical level they also comment on a character forced out of his comfort zone and required to work in favor of the marriage plot instead of against it.

The displacement of the blocking character role from the old men to the young men is completed in the character of Lesbonicus. I will say more about Lesbonicus in Chapter 3, but here it is sufficient to point out that despite the hints about his character from Callicles, who alleges that Lesbonicus has shattered his father's wealth and dragged him into poverty (108–9), when we actually see Lesbonicus onstage, we are met with a young man who is concerned about the well-being of his friends and family (425–31; 680–5) and anxious for the return of his father (590). Compare this to Philolaches in *Mostellaria*, who, like most comic young men, hopes his father will never return and absolutely panics at news of his arrival. When we meet Lesbonicus, for a moment it seems that we will get the double love plot that is so common in Terence and which Terence likely took from Menander. But contrary to our expectations, Lesbonicus has no specific love interest and thus needs no comic scheming to secure his access to her. Anderson suggests that Plautus has removed Lesbonicus' love interest from Philemon's Greek original in order to make the play intentionally boring.[19] Regardless of what may or may not have been in Philemon's version, Plautus does not spoil the play here. Instead, he does something rather daring—he makes the young man into the blocking character. Since the old men have vacated this responsibility in favor of comic scheming, someone must step in and provide the conflict in the play. Enter Lesbonicus, who becomes the obstacle that needs to be overcome for Lysiteles' wedding to proceed. When Philto first broaches the subject of the marriage with him, Lesbonicus flatly refuses and even accuses Philto of mocking the indigent circumstances of his family (445–53). When Lesbonicus finally assents to the marriage, he insists that it will not be without a dowry, and when he and Lysiteles argue over this point, the two young men end up parting ways without coming to a compromise (627–716). For the marriage to succeed, the other characters must find some way to provide a dowry for Lesbonicus' sister and thus overcome her brother's objections to the marriage. Although we have arrived here in a roundabout way, this much at least fits the typical comic plot—money must be procured for the love affair/marriage to succeed. Since the old men are all in favor of the match, Lesbonicus is forced to transform into a most improbable comic character—a stern young man [*adulescens durus*] who prevents rather than facilitates the love plot.

Trickster Wanted

Shawn O'Bryhim explains how the displacement of one stock character from his typical role can often cause further displacements in the play, setting off a chain reaction that leaves characters struggling to find where they fit in.[20] This is exactly what happens to Lesbonicus' enslaved sidekick Stasimus, who ends up bouncing around between two stereotypical slave personae: the clever slave [*servus callidus*] and the faithful slave [*servus fidelis*], even throwing in a running slave shtick at the end [*servus currens*]. Before Lesbonicus hears about the marriage proposal and settles firmly into his role as blocking character, Stasimus gives the appropriate cues that he will be playing the clever slave, unaware, as he is, that the old men have already reserved this responsibility for themselves. When Lesbonicus and Stasimus first enter, they discuss the miserable state of Lesbonicus' finances in an exchange that is full of the snarky riposte and inverted social dynamic that is to be expected in scenes between the young lover and the clever slave (402–31, cf. *Pseudolus* 1–131).[21] Stasimus criticizes his young master's financial choices, especially his decision to serve as guarantor for a friend's loan (425–31), and even brags that he stole some of the money from the sale of the house (413). During the ensuing conversation with Philto about the marriage proposal, Stasimus frequently interrupts to present his own opinions, much to Lesbonicus' chagrin (e.g., 463–5). All of these are behaviors that can be expected from the clever slave character.

The closest that Stasimus gets to playing the clever slave is in a miniaturized version of a deception plot at lines 515–61. Lesbonicus has just offered to give away the family farm, the last real possession left to him, as a dowry for his sister. Fearing the financial ruin this will cause for the family, Stasimus decides that something must be done, and he is just the person to do it. "We are clearly done for, unless I can come up with something," he exclaims (515–16). The verb I translated as "come up with something," *comminiscor* in Latin, is a verb that Plautus frequently employs for marking comic scheming, as when Jupiter tells

Mercury to deceive Amphitruo in any way that he can (*Amph*. 979) or when Periplectomenus praises Palaestrio's plan to pretend his master's girlfriend has a twin sister (*Miles* 241; see also *Asin*. 102). Stasimus' plot is somewhat less spectacular. Rather than orchestrating a complex play-within-a-play, as Mercury and Palaestrio do in the previous examples, Stasimus instead pulls Philto aside and tells him that the farm is bad—like really, really bad. That's it.[22] Lame, I know, but to be fair, Stasimus' description does include some humorous moments, like when he nonchalantly tells Philto that there is a gateway to hell on the property (525) and then claims that every other tree has been struck by lightning (539); however, the funniest aspect of the scene is its sense of metatheatrical disappointment. When the scheme wraps up less than fifty lines in, the audience member who is well-accustomed to Plautine trickery asks, "Is that it?" Stasimus confirms that that is indeed all there is, when he announces in an aside to the audience that he has "cleverly terrified the old man away from the farm" (560). The word translated as cleverly is *lepide* in Latin, an adverbial form of the adjective *lepidus* which, like *comminiscor*, is used to highlight comic deception in Plautus.[23]

In a later scene, after Lesboncius and Lysiteles fail to come to an agreement over the dowry (627–716), Stasimus gets one final chance to play the trickster. It is clear that someone has to come up with a plan to procure money for the dowry in order for the marriage plot to succeed. The young men storm off the stage in an impasse, leaving Stasimus alone to soliloquize. This is certainly the moment in which he will rise to his comic potential. He addresses himself in the vocative case, "Stasimus, you stand alone!" (*Stasime, restas solus*, 718), just like the quintessential comic schemer Pseudolus does in his play (*tu astas solus, Pseudole*, 394). It is at this moment that Pseudolus so clearly proclaims the metatheatrical potential of the clever slave [*servus callidus*]. "Now, I will become a poet," he confidently announces (*nunc ego poeta fiam*, 404), signaling to the audience that he will take over as playwright and craft a deception plot that will write him and his young master Calidorus out of peril.[24] What does Stasimus say in a nearly identical moment?

> Stasimus, you stand alone. What should I do now,
> except hitch up my satchel, slap a shield on my back,
> and get some tragic heels added to these comic slippers?
> It can't be stopped.
>
> 718-20

When faced with the opportunity to write the play-within-a-play, Stasimus turns it down and leaves himself at the mercy of the events unfolding around him! Compare this to Pseudolus, who promises the audience that through his clever scheming he will create a pile of cash out of thin air: "Those twenty minas, / though they don't exist anywhere on earth right now, nevertheless I will find them!" (*Pseud.* 404–5). Typical Plautine tricksters would never say, as Stasimus does here, "It can't be stopped," (*non sisti potest*, 720), because they are the ones who fashion the onstage reality for the other characters. This little half-line, more than any other, signals to the audience that Stasimus will not play the usual *servus callidus* role nor will he challenge the old men for control of the deception plot.

The attentive audience member probably already figured this out from previous hints about Stasimus' conflicted identity. Despite Stasimus' eagerness to party with Lesbonicus and even steal money from him, the purpose of his mini deception with Philto concerning the farm was to protect the property of his old master Charmides in his absence, a behavior more typical of the faithful slave character [*servus fidelis*]. Stasimus shows this side of his character again when he wishes for the safe return of Charmides as father of the household (617–19), an event that is usually disastrous for the young men and their clever slaves in comedy. Throughout the play, Stasimus toys with the identity of the faithful slave, but doesn't fully commit to that persona either.

When Stasimus returns at the end of the play (1008–114), he can't play the trickster character because the old men have already executed their play-within-a-play, and he can't be a proper *servus fidelis* because Charmides has defeated the sycophant and doesn't need his help any longer. What is there left for Stasimus to do? Why not try out the running slave bit! We will examine this scene in more detail in Chapter 5, but the pertinent thing here is that Stasimus does a marvelous running slave entrance, replete with ironic moralizing and a comic refusal to recognize the people he is looking for. Once the truth about the house, the treasure, the dowry, and the marriage are revealed to everyone, Charmides sends Stasimus off on an errand that is unnecessary for the plot but does give Stasimus a chance to do a humorous running slave exit. "Run at full speed to the Piraeus and do it all in one lap," Charmides orders (1102–3). Cue the wild elbows, hitched-up tunic, and clumsy dash through the audience. This is certainly one of those moments in which the text gives us only a glimpse of the potential for physical humor on the Plautine stage.

Over the course of the play, Stasimus jumps back and forth between playing the clever slave, the faithful slave, and the running slave, in the end doing a poor job at each of these, but when one is familiar with these character types, there is humor in his attempt to cover all the bases and ultimately fall short. Stasimus' stock-character schizophrenia is a result of the old men laying claim to the role of *architecti doli* in the first scene. Stasimus has already been displaced before he even comes onstage.

Old Schemers [*Senes Callidi*]

Now we have come to the part of the play where a deception of some sort is needed to produce the money necessary for the marriage plot to succeed. Re-enter the old men Megaronides and Callicles who now fully embrace the role of *arcitecti doli* (729–819). After a brief discussion, they conclude that Lesbonicus' sister must have a dowry and that they must provide it immediately. Of course, the money is already in Callicles' possession in the treasure that is hidden in Charmides' house, but he worries that if he digs it up Lesbonicus will find out about the money and spend it on frivolities rather than on his sister's nuptials. Callicles' initial inclination is to solve the problem as any well-connected Athenian (or Roman) gentleman would—just ask a friend for a loan.

Megaronides, however, hasn't forgotten that they are in a comedy, and he instead presents a proper deception plot:

> **Meg** I have found a **clever plan** [*scitum. . .consilium*], as I see it.
>
> **Cal** What is it?
>
> **Meg** Some guy is to be hired, as soon as possible, as if he were from abroad. **CAL** What does he know how to do after that?
>
> **Meg** He ought to be all dressed up **just right** [*graphice*] in foreign fashion with an unknown appearance, the kind not seen around here, someone who spouts off deceptions—
>
> **Cal** What does he know how to do after that?
>
> **Meg** —a fabricator of fraud, a real confidence man—**CAL** Ooh! What next?
>
> **Meg** —as if he is coming to the young man from his father in Seleucia.
>
> 763–73

Like a playwright taking charge, Megaronides outlines the play-within-a-play with specifications for the type of actor that should be chosen to play the conman and the costume he should wear. In the following lines, he goes on to describe the necessary props: two letters written as if from Charmides, one to Callicles and one to Lesbonicus, announcing that Charmides has allegedly sent money from abroad for the dowry, all so that Lesbonicus won't suspect that the money really comes from a treasure hidden inside the house. Finding co-conspirators, costumes, and forged letters for the deception are hallmarks of typical deception scenes in Roman comedy, but here it is the old men who are doing these things, not the clever slaves and their helpers.

As in their earlier scene, the old men here use the language of comic plotting to highlight the metatheatrical aspects of the play within a play that they devise. Megaronides describes the plot as clever [*scitus*], a word also used by Chrysalus and Pseudolus, two of Plautus' most inveterate tricksters, to mark comic scheming in their plays (*Bacch.* 209;

Pseud. 748). Pseudolus and his interlocutor Charinus even use this word to describe the conman that they are hiring to deliver a deceptive letter in their play, a context very similar to this scene in *Trinummus*. At the end of the scene, Callicles reprises his friend's use of this word by calling Megaronides' plan "very clever by Hercules!" (*scite hercle sane*, 783) and "clever and excellent enough!" (*satis scite et probe*, 786). When Megaronides describes how the conman should be dressed, he uses the adverb *graphice* (which I translated as "just right" above), another word associated with comic trickery in Plautus.[25] To drive the point home, Megaronides finishes the scene with further verbal references to Plautine deception plots with his use of the words "charming" [*lepidus*, 809] and "in a very ridiculous fashion" [*nugacissume*, 819], both of which reinforce the playfulness that permeates schemes of deception in Roman comedy.

In this scene, the old men make good on the promise from their first appearance to take charge of the comic deception in the play, thus clearly articulating Plautus' new, experimental character type that he elaborates in *Trinummus*, the clever old man [*senex callidus*].[26] Megaronides is fully committed to playing the trickster, but Callicles is less certain about his new comic responsibilities. He draws attention to the incongruence of his costume and age with his new role by saying, "I am ashamed to be playing the con artist at my age" (*hoc me aetatis sycophantari pudet*, 787), thus making sure that no one misses the shuffling of the usual character types.[27] Just like Philto, who was reluctant to play against type and help arrange his son's marriage, Callicles has doubts about how well a comic deception designed by the old men will work, doubts that turn out to be well founded when the conman's scheme fails to go to plan.

Outconning the Conman

Just when everything seems set up perfectly—letters have been forged, the conman hired, costumes procured, money extracted from the treasure, etc.—Plautus throws us a curve. Immediately following the exit of the old men, Charmides, Lesbonicus' father, unexpectedly arrives home from Seleucia. The arrival of the father on the scene is always a threat to the deception plot and it is no different here, but, in a paradoxical way, Charmides' unlooked-for return also promises to sort everything out with the dowry, the marriage, the house, and the treasure. In fact, it seems that the play could just end right here, if Charmides were to run into his old friend Callicles and hear what has really been going on, but instead it is the conman who meets with Charmides, the one who is bringing letters that are supposedly from Charmides himself. Here we get to what is certainly the funniest scene in the play (go read it out loud with a friend—you'll see!).[28] The humor is primarily predicated on the inversion of expected stock character behaviors. Old men in comedy usually don't stand a chance against the wiles of an imposter like this, but here it is Charmides who outwits the conman.

The conman is unnamed in the manuscripts, labeled only as *sycophanta*, which here means trickster or cheat. During the scene, the conman tells Charmides that his nickname is Pax, not the Latin word meaning peace but rather a Greek exclamation that you say when you

Figure 2.2 Charmides and the conman, from the 1903 production of *Trinummus* at Westminster School. *Black & White*, Dec. 19, 1903. Reproduced by kind assistance of the Governing Body of Westminster School.

want a conversation to be over, like "Enough!"—a fitting sobriquet for a character who makes his living spinning lies. Everything is set up for the conman to succeed, but when faced with the opportunity, he fails, just like Stasimus does when he is given the chance to play the trickster. Again, it is because the old men have already taken control of the play, but here it is the newcomer Charmides who runs things, instead of Megaronides.

Right away, we get hints that the dynamics in the scene are inverted when Charmides opens with a monologue and then hides and eavesdrops on the conman. Monologues, eavesdropping, and asides are the most significant ways that characters in Plautus build rapport with the audience. As Moore points out, "Characters able to address the audience unheard by an interlocutor onstage make a powerful connection with the spectators."[29] Charmides initially establishes this connection with a humorous prayer of thanksgiving to Neptune that he offers along with a monologue describing his return voyage (for more on this prayer, see Chapter 4). When the conman enters, Charmides eavesdrops while the newcomer describes how he was hired and outfitted for this job (840–70). This act of eavesdropping places the characters in a comic hierarchy of rapport with the audience and grants Charmides control over the scene. Charmides has the chance to overhear part of the conman's scheme, including the fact that he doesn't actually know the person from whom he is pretending to bring the letters (848–50), and this information gives the old man a clear advantage in their subsequent encounter. Furthermore, Charmides even gets the chance to jest about the conman's trumped-up foreign appearance, commenting on his Illyrian complexion and traveling hat that makes him look like a mushroom (851–2). Thus, by the time the two characters finally address each other, Charmides has already established a strong upper hand.

Throughout the scene, Charmides maintains his advantage through constant asides to the audience, which strengthen his rapport with them as well as undermine the conman's position. Over the course of 127 lines (870–997), Charmides delivers nine asides to the audience, none of which are overheard or commented on by the conman.[30] The conman does acknowledge two of the asides by requesting that Charmides pay attention to what he is saying, but he never acknowledges the content of the asides or the fact that Charmides is interacting with the audience. The conman, in turn, has only two asides, back to back in lines 911 and 912, the second of which Charmides comments on. The balance of asides to the audience in the scene gives further advantage to Charmides.

As the scene progresses, the conman tells Charmides that he is bringing letters to Lesbonicus and Callicles from Lesbonicus' father, whom he alleges is his friend and traveling companion, unaware that the man he is addressing is actually Lesbonicus' father Charmides. This opens the door for several humorous moments, like when the conman says that his friend Charmides is six inches taller than the actual Charmides (903–4). The best moment, however, is when the conman forgets Charmides' name and has to be reminded of it by Charmides himself. The actors draw it out for a good twenty lines, and they could have extended it even more in performance through improv if the audience were responding well (905–27).[31] After a guessing game in which Charmides presents all the C names he can think of besides his own, the conman finally recognizes the name when Charmides tells it to him. This moment of the name guessing, more than any other in the scene, marks Charmides' victory and the conman's ultimate inability to play his typical stock role.

For a comparison that shows what the sycophant character in Plautus is normally capable of, we can look at *Pseudolus* 982–91.[32] Here the clever slave Pseudolus has hired a con artist to pretend to be Harpax, a messenger from a braggart soldier who has been sent with a letter and final payment to fetch a woman whom the soldier purchased from the pimp Ballio. Pseudolus' plan is to use the letter and the disguise to steal the woman for his master Calidorus. Since Ballio already knows Pseudolus, Pseudolus can't perpetrate the deception himself, but instead he has to watch from the wings as the conman Simia pretends to be Harpax, with Pseudolus all the while commenting to the audience on the action. When Ballio asks the pseudo-Harpax the name of the soldier,

Pseudolus panics because he realizes that he hasn't actually given Simia this information. Simia, however, handles the moment expertly by asking Ballio to recognize the seal on the letter and provide the soldier's name as proof that Ballio really is who he says he is. Thus, Simia is able to maintain control of the scene and overcome a lack of knowledge through his expert improvisational skills.

The conman in *Trinummus* is in a very similar situation when Charmides asks the name of the man who gave him the letter. When faced with the opportunity, like Simia, to display the prowess of his character type, he instead falls short, forgetting that a proper Plautine trickster never needs real information to succeed—he just makes it up as he goes! The name that the conman gives to Charmides, Pax, is even similar to the name Harpax in *Pseudolus*. Could this be a metatheatrical way for Plautus to signal that Pax in *Trinummus* is only half the conman that the renowned Harpax/Simia of *Pseudolus* is? Just like how Stasimus echoes Pseudolus' famous monologue when he has the chance to take control of the intrigue plot but fails, Pax echoes the expert deception of Harpax/Simia, but also fails to wrest control of the deception from the old men in the play. Given the similarities between the monologues of Stasimus and Pseudolus discussed above, and the connection between the names Pax and Harpax, it is possible that Plautus is signaling to his viewers that they are supposed to compare the inverted character types of *Trinummus* to the specimens par excellence that he presents us with in *Pseudolus*. For this allusion to work, we would need to assume de Melo's later date of 188–187 BCE for *Trinummus*, since we know that *Pseudolus* premiered in 191 BCE at the games for the Great Mother Goddess [*ludi Megalenses*].

As the scene continues, Charmides attempts to push his advantage too far. When he hears that the conman is claiming to bring money from "his friend Charmides," the real Charmides decides that he will try to swindle Pax out of the money, boldly claiming in an aside to the audience that he plans to "outcon the conman" (958). It is a nice idea, but Charmides' plan to get the money consists of merely revealing his true identity. "Give me the money ... I am Charmides," he boldly proclaims

(968, 970). The conman, however, is having none of it: "Get out of here you cheat! Are you really trying to cheat a cheater?" (972). Pax goes on to point out that Charmides didn't reveal his identity until after hearing about the money. "Just like you Charmidized yourself, you can go ahead and un-Charmidize yourself" (977). After some strenuous insistence, Charmides finally convinces the conman of his identity, but it doesn't matter because the conman doesn't actually have the money. In the end, Charmides proves to be the cleverest of the clever old men in the play by overturning the deception plot set in motion by Megaronides and Callicles, but even in his victory he shows the incongruity of having the old man play the trickster. On the streets of Rome or Athens (or London or LA) the wealthy, well-connected men get what they want by merely proclaiming who they are, handing over a business card as it were, but in the topsy-turvy world of the Plautine stage, schemes of deception never succeed by revealing your true identity! The old men make poor *architecti doli* because they don't understand that success in a comic intrigue can never be attained by playing yourself.

In addition to the failure of Charmides to fully outcon the conman, this scene also marks the failure of Megaronides' scheme to get a dowry to Lesbonicus' sister. Unlike in other plays, however, the failure of the deception plot does not mean the failure of the proposed marriage/love affair, since Charmides' return holds the keys to sorting everything out.[33] On a metatheatrical level, a deception schemed up by the aristocratic old men was bound to fail from the start because they already control the necessary resources, both in the world of the play and in real life. By contrast, when the *servus callidus* puts his schemes into action, it is compelling because he usually has nothing to work with besides his intellect and ability to craft his wily dreams into comic reality. Although the scheme of Megaronides and Callicles fails, there is no negative repercussion for them because they didn't have to go all in on their wager, unlike, for example, Tranio in *Mostellaria*, who ends up taking refuge at the stage altar when his scheme explodes (1076–121). When the deception fails in *Trinummus*, we are just able to get to the denouement faster.

The eventual failure of the plot of the old men may have even been signaled by the way their scenes of scheming sounded to the audience. Plautus wrote in many different meters and his plays can be broken down into sections that are accompanied and unaccompanied, usually with some degree of song and dance in the accompanied sections. According to Timothy Moore, scenes of comic plotting in Roman comedy are usually written in a meter called trochaic septenarii, which would have been accompanied by music and involved singing. Megaronides' scenes, however, are written in iambic senarii, the unaccompanied, spoken meter. So, although Megaronides employs language and motifs of comic scheming in his scenes, they would have sounded wrong to the audience—the usual trickster's soundtrack was missing![34] (See Appendix A for a complete analysis of the music in *Trinummus*.)

Actors and Roles in *Trinummus*

Given the wit displayed by Charmides in his confrontation with the conman and the way he asserts control over the scene by maintaining a strong rapport with the audience, it is almost as if Megaronides is back onstage running the show. In a way, that may actually have been the case. Because of economic considerations, actors in Roman comedy usually played more than one role in any given play, though it was uncommon for actors to share roles (i.e., one role played by multiple actors in the course of a play).[35] The total number of actors required for a given play is determined by the scene that requires the largest number of actors present onstage at the same time. For *Trinummus*, this is the final scene, which requires four actors to play Charmides, Callicles, Lysiteles, and Lesbonicus. Since Stasimus appears with each of these characters at other points in the play, we can raise the total number of actors for *Trinummus* to five. By going through the play, scene by scene, and analyzing who appears onstage with whom, it is possible to make a chart that indicates which roles can be played by the same actor. It is also helpful to include adjacent entrances and exits in this list as well, since actors typically required about ten lines to make a costume change backstage. Also, the division of roles and lines in any given play tended to favor one or two star actors, rather than distributing the lines evenly throughout the troupe. The star roles in a Roman comedy usually focus on the characters who manage the deception plot, often the clever slaves like Pseudolus and Chrysalus (*Bacchides*).[36]

When we do this for *Trinummus*, we see that initially there isn't one clear star role in the play based on the total number of lines, but when we start combining roles based on similar themes between the characters, some interesting possibilities emerge. Table 2.4 shows a possible breakdown of the roles in *Trinummus* by actor. *Trinummus* is unique among Plautus' scripts in that there are many possibilities for dividing up the roles between the five actors. It is easier to say which roles cannot be played by the same actor than to say definitively that two roles had to be played by the same person. For example, we can say for certain that the same actor could not have played Stasimus and Lesbonicus, since they are frequently onstage together. It is more difficult to say for certain that the Stasimus actor also played the conman, but there are certain interpretive benefits to breaking the actors and roles down in this way, as I will explain.

If one actor were to play Megaronides, Philto, and Charmides, then the clever, garrulous, and moralizing aspects of the old men in the play would be focused on the same actor, who gets to take on the challenge of turning the old men into the tricksters. This would likely be done by the

Table 2.4 Potential actor–role divisions in *Trinummus*

Actor 1 (star)	Actor 2 (star)	Actor 3	Actor 4	Actor 5
Megaronides	Stasimus	Lesbonicus	Callicles	Lysiteles
Philto	Conman			
Charmides*	Inopia			
Luxuria*	(Curculio actor? See Chapter 5)			
* requires lightning costume change				

actor who usually played the clever slave [*servus callidus*] in other plays. Megaronides and Philto share a heavy dose of ironic moralizing (see Chapter 5 for more on this topic), while Charmides and Megaronides both build rapport with the audience through monologues, eavesdropping, and comic scheming. If one actor were to play both Charmides and Megaronides, it would require a lightning costume change between lines 819 and 820. While difficult, it would not be impossible to execute such a costume change, especially since it would only require adding traveling attire to an actor already dressed as an old man. While Luxuria could be played by any of the actors, adding this role to the list of Actor 1 would emphasize the wealth and resources that the old men control in the play, at the cost of adding one more lightning costume change. A brief pause after the prologue to carry out this change may be warranted by the aesthetic unity that this role-sharing scheme would provide. The lightning costume changes, while difficult to execute, may actually be factors in favor of this assignment of roles, since they provide the star actor with one more avenue to display his virtuosity.

The second actor could play the roles of Stasimus and the conman. These roles go together well because these are the characters who should be in control throughout the play but fall short of their potential and ultimately yield to the clever old men. It would be easy to add Inopia to this actor's list of roles since she has only one line at the beginning of the play, though again, this role could be assigned to anyone. Where Luxuria symbolizes the wealth and power that the old men possess, Inopia can represent the lack of financial and comic resources from which Stasimus and the conman suffer; therefore, assigning this role to Actor 2 would increase the thematic resonances in the play.

Conclusion: *Trinummus* as Experimental Theater

Sophia Papaionannou calls *Trinummus* experimental theater, arguing that in this play we see Plautus attempting to invert the generic expectations of Roman comedy that he himself helped to establish.

"The effectiveness of this strategy," she explains, "depended upon the audience's anticipation, even expectation of being surprised, and upon their ability to identify the routine that is reversed and assess it in comparison to possible earlier treatments of the same routine."[37] Over the course of this chapter, I hope you have received enough background in the typical characters and plot arcs of Roman comedy to recognize, assess, and compare the inverted games that Plautus plays with the characters of *Trinummus*. All these inversions are set in motion when the old men claim the trickster role at the outset. This forces Lysiteles to speak like a blocking character and Lesbonicus to act as one, for the sake of providing conflict for the plot. This also puts Stasimus out of a job as clever slave, leaving him to experiment with the roles of faithful slave and running slave. When the conman enters the scene, he is soundly defeated by Charmides, who proves to be the cleverest of the old men in the play. The humor in *Trinummus* comes not so much from the situation itself as from the distance between the audience's expectation and what they actually get on the stage. From Plautus' comic laboratory of *Trinummus* we see new, hybrid character types issuing forth: the clever old man [*senex callidus*], the stern young man [*adulescens durus*], and the feckless slave/conman [*servus/sycophanta inops*].

So, if *Trinummus* is experimental, we must ask ourselves, does the experiment succeed? Well, that is up to you to decide, but now, just like Plautus' Roman audience, you have the necessary context in the characters, scenes, and storylines of Roman comedy to make that decision for yourselves.

3

What's Roman about *Trinummus*?

Plautus Vortit Barbare: Roman Comedy and Greek Originals

Plautus and the other authors of Roman comedy adapted their scripts from Greek plays that had been written approximately a century earlier. While there is certainly a strong relationship between the Roman and the Greek texts in question, we would be wrong to think of these new Roman plays merely as literary translations of prior Greek material. The process of moving from the genre we call Greek New Comedy to Roman comedy [*fabula palliata*] involved a mixture of translation, dramatic adaptation, and authorship of new material. What exactly was changed from the Greek to the Roman and how the quality of the latter compared to the former has been a topic of endless debate, and rightly so, for one simple reason: with one exception, the Greek models of Plautus' comedies have not survived. A papyrus fragment of Menander's *Dis Exapaton*, first published and discussed in 1968 by E. W. Handley, provides us with two scenes from the play on which Plautus' *Bacchides* is based.[1] A side-by-side comparison of the two reveals that Plautus changed the characters involved, added musical accompaniment and stylistic flourishes, transposed scenes within the play, and even deleted entire speeches while adding others—a far cry indeed from simple translation![2] But at the same time, this solitary parallel example only provides us with about fifty lines of comparative material for one play. It is a tantalizing case study, but one that begs the question, is this play typical or unique in the world of Plautine adaptation? For that matter, we also ought to ask how Plautus' practice compared to that of his contemporaries whose texts have not survived. A myriad of unanswered (and unanswerable) questions arises regarding the relationship between Roman comedy and its Greek models, but that of course does not mean that scholars haven't tried.

One of the challenges with addressing this relationship is that, for a long time, the texts of Plautus were studied primarily as a way to access the lost Greek plays on which they were based. The reasons for this have more to do with the culture and politics of nineteenth-century Europe than they do with the relative merits of Roman versus Greek literature, but whatever the reasons, an emphasis on lost Greek originals ignores the fact that a Roman audience viewing a play performed in Rome would have created a particularly Roman meaning from that play, regardless of how closely the play translated or followed its Greek original. For *Trinummus*, the more interesting question to ask of the play is not how it compared to the lost Greek play on which it was based (Philemon's *Thensauros*), but rather what in *Trinummus* would have resonated with a Roman audience given the historical and cultural context of the early second century BCE. Before addressing this question, I first want to explain why this and similar questions have not yet been thoroughly explored for Plautine drama, and to do this, we must make a brief detour into the overall history of classical scholarship and scholarship on ancient drama over the last two centuries. By examining the cultural assumptions and biases that hindered the appreciation of Roman comedy in its Roman context, we will be better equipped to explore the trajectory for Plautine studies in the future.

The early nineteenth century saw the rise of a new way of analyzing the Latin and Greek texts that serve as our portal into the ancient world. Coming on the heels of the scientific revolution that swept Europe in the eighteenth century, German scholars of Latin and Greek began looking for more methodical ways of analyzing these languages than the humanistic practices that proliferated in southern Europe during the Renaissance.[3] Christian Gottlob Heyne and Johann Joachim Winckelmann were pioneers in their systematic treatment of ancient texts, but it would be Heyne's student Friedrich August Wolf who would finally give a name to this new, professionalized approach to classical philology: *Altertumswissenschaft* [the Science of Antiquity] which entailed the formal study of all aspects of the ancient Mediterranean world.[4] Wolf published his most influential work, *Prolegomena ad Homerum*, in 1795, in which he combined techniques of textual analysis with historical inquiry into the composition of Homer's *Iliad* and *Odyssey*, inaugurating a debate about the origins of epic poetry that would come to be known as the Homeric Question.[5] In particular, Wolf argued that the two poems could not have been written by a single author and he used textual analysis to identify what he saw as the various constituent parts of the poems—in essence a search for the sources of Homer's texts. Wolf's findings, many of which were refuted in the ensuing years, were ultimately not as influential as his innovative methods of inquiry, in which he employed close textual analysis in support of historical arguments. A major component of this more scientific approach to classical literature, as indicated in Wolf's *Prolegomena*, was the "search for the sources of texts," an academic endeavor that also received an appropriately German name, *Quellenforschung*.[6]

Part and parcel with the new German classicism came a tendency to value Greek culture, art, and texts over Roman material. Since, in many ways, Roman art and literature developed in response to Greek models, Winckelmann and Wolf saw the Roman material as derivative and used it primarily as a vehicle for approaching what they saw as superior in Greek culture.[7] This predilection for all things Greek developed in the early nineteenth century into a cultural phenomenon called philhellenism. The Greek war of independence in the 1820s and 30s put a practical face on the growing intellectual movement of philhellenism and helped fuel the growth of the romantic myth of ancient Greece as the pristine birthplace of modern Europe. The expanding philhellenic fervor, sometimes referred to derogatorily as Graecomania, became the equivalent of a pop culture phenomenon during the mid-1800s throughout Europe and the United States, with lasting effects in political, academic, and social arenas in the form of Greek-inspired political liberalism, educational reforms, and popular music and theater.[8]

The increasing popularity of philhellenism and the expansion of the new German model of classical studies (*Altertumswissenschaft*) had a reciprocal effect on each other—classical studies appeared to have an obvious cultural relevance, while philhellenism led scholars to focus on Greek texts, sometimes to the detriment of Roman ones. The study of ancient drama as we know it, including Plautine studies, came into its own amid this ideological mixture of philology, philhellenism, and *Quellenforschung*. During the 1800s, scholars possessed only fragments of Greek New Comedy (the source material for Plautus) mostly in the form of passages quoted by other authors. Significant papyrus fragments of Menander would not be discovered and published until 1907, with more discoveries and publications appearing through the 1960s.[9] However, in the full spirit of philhellenism, scholars of the late 1800s were certain that the Greek models must have been far superior to the surviving Roman copies. After all, all things Greek are pristine and beautiful, and all things Roman are, well, rather Roman. Furthermore, they had assurances from critics from antiquity, such as Aristophanes of Byzantium (*fl. c.* 200 BCE), that writers of Greek New Comedy, like Menander, were, to put it simply, really good. "O Menander and Life," Aristophanes was quoted as saying, "which of you imitates which?" (Syrianus, *Comm. in Herm.* 23.7). According to the canons of the time, what higher praise could there be of art than that it flawlessly imitated (Greek) life?

So, given this unfortunate hand dealt by fate concerning the surviving corpus of ancient comedy, there was only one logical thing to do, from the philhellenic perspective: use analysis of "inferior" Roman comedy to reconstruct the "superior" Greek originals. Thus, much of the early analysis of Plautine drama was not undertaken to understand it in its own right, but rather in an attempt to recover texts that were irretrievably lost. This approach is exemplified in the works of scholars such as Friedrich Leo, Eduard Fraenkel, and Gunther Jachmann. While these works are remarkable for the depth of their authors' understanding and engagement with the Plautine corpus, they ultimately suffer from what Duckworth calls "the unfounded assumption of the perfection of Attic comedy and ... the accompanying theory of the faultiness of Roman workmanship."[10] For example, Leo, in *Plautinische Forschungen* (1895), sums up his position on the question in the introduction to his chapter titled, "Plautus and his original," when he says, "The standard judgment of Plautus gives him both too much and too little credit. His comedies are not his and they were more beautiful and better before he made them his own, but his style developed on his own soil, although it was transplanted from a foreign land."[11]

Fraenkel's *Plautinisches im Plautus* (1922, available in English translation as *Plautine Elements in Plautus*, tr. Muecke 2007) is a monument in Plautine studies and Fraenkel is well known for his careful analysis of the plays in order to find things that Plautus clearly added to his adaptations, such as an expanded role for the clever slave character. While Fraenkel's work on Plautus has arguably been foundational for modern studies of Roman comedy, he does reveal his own philhellenic biases against Roman literature in phrases such as, "We must not imagine [Plautus] was capable...of thinking up elements of a main plot by himself."[12] Jachmann, who built on the work of Fraenkel, follows suit, as is apparent in Beare's review of Jachmann's *Plautinisches und Attisches* (1931), in which he describes Jachmann's engagement with the *Quellenforschung* school of Plautine studies in the following way:

> In his attempt to strip off the "curling stucco-work" of Plautine accretions and reveal the Attic columns underneath, slender, straight and graceful, [Jachmann] takes as his basic principle the high technical excellence of the νέα κωμῳδία[New Comedy, i.e., Greek originals]. In the Greek play, speech and action form an organic whole; no detail is inserted merely for its own sake; elements of unreality there are, but the inconceivabilities of the Latin plays are laid to the account of the Latin playwright.[13]

Lest we think that there is some irony in Beare's statement, he follows it up with this evaluation: "The intricate and cautious argument yields striking results." Farther on in the review, Beare expresses the logical conclusion of this line of argument when he refers to Plautus' *Aulularia* (as analyzed by Jachmann) as "Menander's masterpiece." Plautus disappears as author entirely, serving only as delivery boy for the delicious Greek original, sans its cellophane wrapping of Plautine accretions (to Beare's credit, he does admit that some will take issue with the principle of "Attic perfection of technique," but in this review, he appears not to). The eventual destination along this line of thinking is expressed by Gilbert Norwood, who claims that Plautus wrote his plays with all the delicacy of "a blacksmith mending a watch," and that the Plautine corpus can rightly be considered a "wilderness of bad construction, cheap characterization, and at times miraculously stupid dialogue."[14] As can be seen from the judgment of these scholars, the cultural and scholarly movements of philhellenism and *Quellenforchung* had a real effect on how the study of Roman comedy developed.

This origin story for Plautine studies has cast a long shadow over the field and it still inflects the types of questions that scholars ask about these plays. For *Trinummus*, William S. Anderson has argued that Plautus took a play from Philemon that featured "a complex plot in which deep ethical commitments were inextricably bound up with love themes," and made it purposefully boring in order to prove that moralizing is futile. In Anderson's view, scenes are "savagely altered by Plautus," and one character, Lysiteles, goes from experiencing deep love and poignant feelings in Philemon's play to "becom[ing] an insufferable prig" and "dwindl[ing] into a self-righteous pompous ass."[15] Remember, of course, that we possess no fragments of Philemon's *Thensauros*—the argument rests entirely on the assumption that the Greek play was good and the Roman play was not. Such a negative assumption about a work of art, in principle, is not the correct place to begin any analysis of it. If we are to understand what the social and cultural impact of Plautine drama was that ensured its survival over millennia, we first have to stop blaming Plautus for not being Greek and instead examine what the appropriation of Greek drama for the Roman stage meant in the context of the expanding imperialist power of Rome in the second century BCE.

One way to move toward a more nuanced and less biased analysis of the relationship between Roman comedy and its Greek predecessors is to use Linda Hutcheon's theory of adaptation. Hutcheon argues that adaptations are acknowledged and extended intertextual engagements with recognizable models. In her view, adaptation is an act of creative and interpretive artistry in its own right that can stand on its own merits: "adaptation is a derivation that is not derivative—a work that is second without being secondary."[16] Frequently, adaptations require that a narrative move across large expanses of time and space in order to be adapted into a new language and cultural context, processes that Hutcheon terms transculturation and indigenization.[17] Terms like these can provide us with more neutral ways of discussing the differences between Greek New Comedy and the Roman *palliatae*. In fact, Hutcheon notes that the vitriol frequently aimed by critics at adaptations results from a misunderstanding of what adaptations are really trying to do, an assumption that the goal of an adaptation is always to reproduce the adapted text faithfully, thus denying the interpretive power of adaptation. For Plautus (and much of Latin literature for that matter), the relationship with Greek models is a mixture of homage and competition, a combination summed up neatly by the Latin term *aemulatio*, which indicates both imitation and rivalry. Looking at adaptations as adaptation and not as some sort of literary parasites or darkened mirrors through which to view lost originals can move us toward a clearer understanding of the merits of Roman comedy when understood in its own context.

As is often the case for an author whose works have become isolated by the vagaries of literary survival, the texts of Plautus themselves frequently provide us with the best evidence for evaluating and understanding the process of adaptation from Greek New Comedy to Roman comedy. The prologue to Plautus' *Trinummus* provides us with a good example of the type of information that these plays tend to provide about the process of adaptation.[18] In her prologue, the goddess Luxuria says:

The name of this play in Greek is *The Treasure* [*Thesauro*]:
Philemon wrote it, Plautus turned it barbarian [*vortit barbare*].

> He made its name *Three Coins* [*Trinummo*]. Now he asks you
> to allow this play to bear this name.
>
> 18–21

On the surface, this mention in the prologue tells us that Plautus acknowledged the Greek model and thought it important to communicate this information to his audience. As Hutcheon points out, acknowledgment of the model is an important part of what constitutes an adaptation.[19] As we dig deeper, we see that Plautus refers to his act of translation and adaptation as "turning the play barbarian." An entire world of complex cultural interactions is tied up in these three words: *Plautus vortit barbare*. As early as the sixth century BCE, the Romans had begun interacting with the Greek colonies of southern Italy (called by the Romans *Magna Graecia*), including appropriating Greek mythology and religion.[20] In the century preceding Plautus' career, the Romans gained hegemony over mainland Italy (Pyrrhic War, 280–275; capture of Tarrentum, 272) and Sicily (First Punic War, 264–241), thus transforming their relationship with the Greeks into one of imperial expansionism.[21] As a result of this extended encounter with a highly literate and artistically sophisticated culture, the Romans moved from territorial to cultural appropriation, which first began with Livius Andronicus' adaptations of Greek epic poetry and drama into Latin, starting in 240 BCE.[22] Roman attitudes toward Greece during the second century BCE became increasingly bipolar: art, literature, and rhetoric continued to develop along decidedly Greek lines, while at the same time anti-Hellenic elements in Roman society saw Greek culture as corrosive and feminizing, referring to the philhellenes as little Greeklings [*graeculi*]. Roman aristocrats who learned Greek and studied Greek literature, in turn, labeled those of their compatriots uninitiated in the Greek language as barbarians [*barbari*], thus using a Greek term for non-Greeks transliterated into Latin to describe fellow Romans.[23] By using the phrase *vortit barbare* to refer to translation, Plautus playfully alludes to the phil- and anti-Hellenic currents in his own society, while at the same time speaking to larger issues of Roman anxiety of influence and overall sense of cultural belatedness vis-à-vis the Greeks.

Plautus' transformative work as adapter is also apparent in his new Roman title of the play. *Trinummus* combines the Latin words *tres* (three) and *nummus* (coin) to mean three coins or three Roman sesterces, the typical wages for one day's worth of unskilled labor. In the play, the conman receives this fee from Callicles and Megaronides. While this is an admittedly minor event on which to base the title of the play, the significance of the title comes not from its place in the plot but rather in its relation to the Greek title *Thensauros* (The Treasure), the quantitative opposite of the paltry coins of Plautus' title. The plot of *Trinummus* does feature a treasure, but Plautus chooses to draw our attention to the worker's wage instead, creating a purposeful economic inversion. But why does he do this? The following line provides a hint. Plautus asks the audience to accept the new name of the play and the inversion implied, thus implicating them in the act of creation/appropriation. The invitation for the audience to accept the new name of the play is, in turn, an invitation for us as modern readers to examine more closely the role of the Roman audience in making meaning from the play. We need to ask ourselves what the play would have meant to a Roman audience, not what the play means to a modern reader using Plautus as a conduit for accessing lost Greek plays.

When we view *Trinummus* from the perspective of the Romans living in the wake of the Second Punic War, we see that Charmides' household reflects the plight of the typical plebeian family, the father forced abroad as a citizen soldier, while at home the family property is at the mercy of inexperienced young men and greedy neighbors. Although the play is nominally set in Athens, the fact that it is performed at Rome for a Roman audience allows us to make these connections between fictional Greek characters and Roman realities. In fact, it was Cicero who, after comparing his defendant Roscius to a character from one of Caecilius' comedies, said:

> It would surely make no difference to the case whether I named this young man of comedy or someone from the fields of Veii (a town near Rome). For I consider these things to have been invented by the poets

so that we might see our own ways represented in the characters of others and thus a carefully fashioned image of our daily life.

Pro Roscio Amerino 46–7, trans. Leigh[24]

Taking our cue from Cicero, lets now do a close reading of *Trinummus* in its historical context and look for the carefully fashioned images of everyday Roman life that it contains.

Fluctuating Wealth in *Trinummus*

It might initially seem that the years following the Second Punic War, with the removal of the threat of Hannibal from Italy, would be years of renewed prosperity for the Roman lower classes. However, ongoing military conflict outside of Italy and inconsistent or unenforced regulations for land distribution ultimately led to greater inequality. In the late 200s BCE, the protracted war with Hannibal had led to extensive depopulation in southern Italy, which was further intensified by the confiscation of land from Roman allies who had sided with Hannibal during his fifteen-year rampage through the peninsula.[25] This empty land provided an opportunity for veterans, and many of Scipio Africanus' soldiers received land allotments in Apulia and Samnium after the war as a reward for their service (Livy 31.4.1–2). However, land grants such as these did not ensure financial stability per se, especially since the land allotments were gradated in such a way as to reproduce a stratified society in the new settlements, with large allotments for the cavalry and officers on top, but small allotments for the foot soldiers on the bottom, so small in fact that they were not large enough to support self-sustaining farming.[26] Thus, the new colonies offered a promise of peaceful prosperity but in fact preserved in their structure the all-too-familiar anxiety and anguish of a peasant class at the bottom, but now one that had fought and bled for the Republic and felt that they deserved better.

The veteran colonies themselves were not sufficient to use up the vast new tracts of public land (*ager publicus*) that were available after the war. Appian, in his history of the Roman civil wars (1.1.7), explains how, during the Roman conquest of Italy, large tracts of captured land were designated as *ager publicus* and any Roman who wished could farm the land, provided he paid a 10-percent tax on produce and a 20-percent tax on livestock. The idea was that this system would provide a strong supply of citizen soldiers and allies, not to mention a steady source of revenue for the state. It was a good plan, but as Appian goes on to explain, it did not work as expected:

> Wealthy men took over the majority of the undistributed land and were encouraged by the passage of time to think that they would never be evicted. Moreover, they gained possession of adjacent plots and whatever other little parcels were farmed by poor families, sometimes persuading the person to sell, sometimes taking it by force. Thus, they were farming vast acreages instead of small plots and using slaves as farmworkers and herdsmen because free workers could be taken away from agriculture for military service ... Therefore certain powerful men became extremely wealthy ... but the Italian people decreased in numbers and strength since they were hard pressed by poverty, taxes, and military service.
>
> 1.1.7, trans. Shelton

As Jo-Ann Shelton explains, "It is indeed one of the great ironies of history that Roman farmers who went to war to defend their property against a foreign enemy ultimately lost their property to fellow Romans and also lost farming jobs to slaves whom they themselves had helped capture."[27]

In response to this situation, the Romans passed a law sometime during the first third of the second century that limited holdings of *ager publicus* to 500 *iugera* per individual, though the law proved difficult to enforce and was routinely disregarded.[28] With no effective mechanism for controlling the greed of the wealthy and with perpetual military demands on average Roman citizens caused by Rome's ongoing wars in Greece and Asia, the demise of the small Roman farm continued throughout the second century. By the time of Tiberius Gracchus' proposed land reforms of 133 BCE, the conflict over class inequality and land redistribution had reached a point of crisis, but the seeds of that crisis lay in the aftermath of the Second Punic War.

Plautus' *Trinummus* provides its audience with a vivid reflection of these social anxieties about wealth, access to land, and vacillating fortunes, right from the outset, with the visual symbolism of the prologue speaker Luxuria [Luxury] and her daughter Inopia [Destitution]. As they enter at the beginning of the play, the two characters have the following exchange:

> **Lux** Follow me this way, daughter, so that you can fulfill your civic duty [*munus fungaris tuom*].
>
> **Ino** I am following, but I don't know what the purpose/destination/ending [*finem*] may be.
>
> **Lux** (*Pointing to Charmides' house*) Here it is. Look, this is the house. Go inside now.
>
> 1–3

We do not find out who these characters are until lines 8–9, but their costumes would have given the audience a clue about their identity and purpose.[29] In these lines, Luxuria reveals their names with a metatheatrical flourish, claiming that Plautus placed their names on them and wanted it to be so [*Plautus nomen . . . indidit; esse voluit*], which highlights the artifice in the scene and reminds the viewer that it is Plautus as author/adapter who is giving them this key symbol at the outset of the play. Furthermore, Luxuria's phrase "fulfill your civic duty" [*munus fungaris tuom*] in the opening line is particularly Roman, drawn from the language of public office and civic responsibility.[30] Later on in the play, Philto, using the same phrase, notes how this Roman idea of civic duty is directly tied to the possession of wealth (353–4). In this way, Plautus starts the play by encouraging the audience to look for relevant connections to Roman culture rather than emphatically placing the action in a distant, Greek land, as Plautine prologues sometimes do.[31] Luxury then ushers her daughter Destitution into the heart of a seemingly well-to-do home, and the daughter says that she does not know what the outcome of the action will be (2). Thus, in the opening moment of the play, Plautus gives his viewers a forceful visual representation of an anxiety that many of them dealt with in their daily lives—the potential entry of poverty into their households and the uncertainty that comes along with it. Instead of assuring the audience that all will be well in the end and that the money will get where it needs to go (cf. *Aulularia* 23–36), the audience is instead told only that the household money is gone (13) and the outcome is uncertain. This uncertainty is emphasized not only by Destitution's entry into the house, but also by the fact that the audience does not see her leave—poverty stays with the household. This threat informs the conflicts and dynamics between the characters for the rest of the play, as can be seen in the absence of Charmides from his house and family, Lesbonicus' wrangling with his wealthy friends, and the potential loss of the family farm.

The Absence of Charmides

For as instrumental as the prologue is in setting up the primary theme of the play, we do not get a clear exposition of the backstory until the old men Callicles and Megaronides begin discussing the circumstances of Charmides' family, most notably Charmides' absence. While it is true that it is not a military expedition that has forced Charmides' departure, there are obvious similarities between the father's absence and the plight of the average Roman soldier. First, Charmides has departed to the east for an indeterminate amount of time and has left his household in the care of his son, with his neighbor Callicles nearby to assist. It is assumed, on analogy with other comedies like *Mercator*, that Charmides is traveling as a merchant, but this is never explicitly stated.[32] Instead, Callicles tells us that Charmides left town in somewhat dire circumstances:

> After this son of his shattered his father's fortunes
> and he himself saw that he had been dragged down to poverty
> and that his daughter was full grown but unmarried,
> at the same time seeing that his wife, the girl's mother, was dead,

when he was about to leave here for Seleucia,
he entrusted to me his unwed daughter, his entire estate,
and that reprobate son of his.

108–14

The language of wealth and poverty saturates these lines: shattered fortunes [*rem confregit*, 108] dragged into poverty [*ad paupertatem protractum esse*, 109], entrusted his entire estate [*comendavit ... rem suam omnem*, 113–14].[33] The circumstances of Charmides' departure are clear, as is his destination, but his reasons for leaving are not expressed. Seleucia was a Hellenistic Greek city on the Tigris River, and, while in a Greek comedy this could easily be the destination for a merchant, for the Romans in the 190s BCE, the mention of Seleucia would have immediately reminded them of the current war in the east against King Antiochus III of the Seleucid Empire and the absence of many men in their families who had gone to fight in the war.[34]

The characters in the play who do not have the information about the secret treasure hidden in Charmides' house all assume that Callicles is cheating Charmides out of his property in his absence. In the opening scene with the old men, Megaronides shares with Callicles the opinion of the neighborhood:

Haven't you plotted against the very one entrusted to your care?
And the one who did the entrusting, haven't you driven him out
  of his house?
... trust this guy with custody, he'll care for his own bottom line
  better [*suam melius rem gesserit*].

136–7, 139

Later on in the play, Lesbonicus' slave Stasismus even worries that Callicles has been plotting all along to cheat Lesbonicus out of both the house and the farm, thus destroying Charmides' estate for good. Stasimus laments:

I pretty much sense and have sniffed out why that guy was in a
  hurry:

So that he could wheedle Lesbonicus out of the farm, just like he
    wheedled him out of the house.
O master Charmides, right now, while your wealth is being pulled
    to pieces in your absence [*apsenti hic tua res distrahitur tibi*],
If only I could see you returned here safe and sound to take
    revenge on your enemies!

615–19

The portrayal of a father's involuntary absence from home and an inexperienced son left to manage the household in the face of potentially unscrupulous neighbors would have resonated with the experiences of many members of Plautus' audience at Rome.

Lesbonicus and his Wealthy Friends

Now you may be saying to yourself, "Hang on, isn't Lesbonicus to blame for the loss of his father's wealth? He isn't a victim. Hasn't he, the young lover, gotten himself into this mess through his own irresponsible behavior and feckless mismanagement?" That's what comparisons to young lovers throughout the corpus of Roman comedy would suggest, but in *Trinummus*, none of the characters behave according to their type and there are clues in the text that Lesbonicus is perhaps different from his comic counterparts in other plays. True, there are the typical criticisms of his behavior expressed by other characters, but they are all focalized through the wealthy and self-secure. The one exception here is the statement of the goddess Luxuria in the prologue who flatly states, "[Lesbonicus] lost his father's wealth, with me as accomplice" [*is rem paternam me adiutrice perdidit*, 13], but what 18-year-old, then or now, would not be at risk of spoiling his father's finances if left alone to manage them? It's possible that Plautus here is parodying the way that the rich in Rome talked about the poor—it's easy for the wealthy to say the poor are poor because of bad morals. When we look beyond the general insults, like "that delinquent son" [*illum corruptum filium*, 114] and "that degenerate" [*ille ignavos*, 165] "who ate what he had and what he didn't have" [*quin comedit quod fuit, quod non fuit*, 361] and instead search for the details of Lesbonicus' behavior, a different picture emerges.

In the only passage in the play in which Lesbonicus attempts an accounting of his expenditures, we are told that, of the forty minas which he received from Callicles for the sale of the house, less than six minas, or 600 drachmas, were spent on typical comic riotous living (booze, bathhouses, barbecue parties, and brothels, 402–12). Conversely, he spent ten minas or 1,000 drachmas paying off a friend's loan that he co-signed (425–30), almost twice as much as the money he spent on himself. While no one would claim that Lesbonicus displays good fiscal management here, the ability to establish and maintain reciprocal relationships of benefaction was a characteristic of the nobility that those trying to break into higher social classes sought to emulate. The specific details about Lesbonicus' expenditures outlined in this scene undercut the more general, moralizing criticism of his spending habits as expressed elsewhere in the play. Lysiteles even admits at one point to Philto that it is through Lesbonicus' generosity to his friends [*per comitatem*, 333] that he is in financial peril. Lysiteles then goes on to use this same language to express his desire to help Lesbonicus: "It is by virtue of the gods, father, that we have the means to be obliging to others who wish us well" [*aliis qui **comitati simus** benevolentibus*, 355–6].[35] Perhaps Lesbonicus' lack of resources is more due to an attempt to maintain a foothold in a higher social class than it is to a general lack of morals.

Most notably absent from the typical *adulescens* scenario is a specific love interest. There is no female character in the play that is the object of Lesbonicus' affections and expenditures, which makes Lysiteles' criticisms of his pursuit of *amor* ring hollow (666–73). Instead of spending on a specific love interest, Lesbonicus tries to lavish his last remaining resources on his sister's dowry. While this incongruity between the *expected* behavior of the comic lover and Lesbonicus' *actual* behavior has been taken as a sign of sloppy writing on Plautus' part, we should instead see this incongruity as an invitation to dig deeper and see what else Plautus might be telling us.[36]

We find clues for this search in how the various characters in the play describe Lesbonicus' family. When Lysiteles asks his father Philto for permission to marry Lesbonicus' sister without a dowry, he tells his father that he wants to do a favor [*bene volo ego . . . facere*] for a friend of his same age [*amico atque aequali*], a young man from a very prominent family [*adulescenti huic genere summo*, 326–8]. Immediately prior to asking about the marriage, Lysiteles asks his father to remember the kind of family to which Lesbonicus belongs, and Philto responds that Lesbonicus is from the very best [*adprime probo*, 373].[37] From these lines we gather that Lesbonicus comes from a family of high social standing, a family that in the Roman context would be part of the *nobiles*, those whose ancestors had risen to the office of consul or praetor.[38]

Although Philto and Lysiteles see no problem with Lesbonicus' family background, Lesbonicus himself emphasizes a difference in status between his family and Philto's. When Philto first brings up the marriage to him, Lesbonicus accuses the old man of mocking him and his family (445–6). When Philto protests, Lesbonicus explains:

mearum me **rerum** novisse aequom est **ordinem**.
cum vostra nostra non est aequa **factio**.

It is reasonable for me to understand the **status** of my **wealth**.
My **social class** is not equal to your own.

451–2, emphasis added

In the phrase "status of wealth" [*rerum . . . ordinem*], Plautus seems to be referring to the census standing of Lesbonicus' family based on wealth, while "social class" [*factio*] could be a reference to the difference between plebeians and patricians in Roman society.[39] These two groups formed one of the earliest divisions of Roman society—the patricians were the ruling aristocracy, and the plebeians were everyone else. By Plautus' day, the highest military posts and public offices, including consul, were available to plebeians as well as patricians, provided they possessed the wealth necessary to engage in politics at the highest levels.[40] While the distinction between the classes of patrician and plebeian still remained an important locus of identity, the ruling aristocracy became a mixture of wealthy patricians and plebeians known as the *nobiles* [nobles or known men].[41] In Roman voting assemblies, citizens were categorized either according to their family status, as determined by birth, or according to household wealth.[42] The plebeian assembly, for example, consisted only of members of the plebeian class, but they voted on laws (*plebiscita*) that were binding on the entire populace.[43] The assembly used for electing most magistrates, the *comitia centuriata*, was organized based on wealth and allowed the wealthiest classes of citizens to vote first. The same divisions used in this assembly also determined one's status in the citizen army.[44] This mixture of different ways of assessing one's position in society, based on birth or wealth, allowed for different paths to power and influence, but also for ways to lose those same things. A patrician family who fell on hard times could experience reduced political clout as a result of lost wealth,[45] but for everyday Romans, the loss of family wealth, especially in the form of land, could reduce someone to the lowest class of citizens who always voted last, the *proletarii* or *capite censi*. Since voting proceeded only until a majority of the voting classes reached a consensus, relegation to the lower census classes essentially amounted to disenfranchisement (Cicero, *de Re Publica* 2.39).[46]

Plautus does not use the labels patrician and plebeian in the play, but there are additional lines in Lesbonicus' interactions with his wealthy friends that would suggest this class distinction to a Roman audience. A few lines after Lesbonicus' initial refusal of the marriage, Philto accepts the fact that Lesbonicus is of a different social class from him, but he offers the marriage anyway. He even makes a joke about the difference in lines 486–7:

> id optumum esse tute ut sis optumus
> si id nequeas, saltem ut optumis sis proxumus.
>
> It is best for you to be the best,
> but if you are unable, at least be nearest to the best.

In addition to the jingling assonance in these lines, there is some wordplay based on alternate meanings for the words "best" [*optumus*] and "nearest" [*proxumus*]. Besides serving as the superlative form of "good" [*bonus*], the adjective *optumus/optimus* also had a political valence for the Romans, who used this word to refer to the ruling aristocracy, especially the patricians, as can be seen in the term Cicero uses for the aristocratic faction in the conflicts of the late Republic, the *optimates*. *Proxumus/proximus*, in addition to simply meaning closest, can also be used to describe friends or relatives, one's next of kin. While *proximus* is not usually used of relatives by marriage, that seems to be the point of the joke here. Given these alternate translations, another way of rendering these lines could be: "It's best to be a patrician/aristocrat, but if you can't do that, at least be related to one." In case the point were lost on anyone in the audience, Philto uses the language of wealth-based social classes in lines 493–4, when he points out that in death both the rich and poor are assessed in the same class [*aequo ... censetur censu*]. Despite Philto's jovial offer, Lesbonicus, for his part, continues to feel inferior to Philto in both his family's wealth and social standing, and so he rejects the marriage.

The most compelling evidence for Lesbonicus' connection to the plebeian class comes when Lesbonicus and Lysiteles are arguing about the dowry. Lysiteles loses his temper and tells Lesbonicus what he really thinks about his behavior:

> Did your ancestors pass down this reputation to you
> so that you, through your disgrace, could lose the things
>   previously provided by their virtue? And, to enable you to
>   assert your children's claim to office,
> your father and your grandfather have made the road to attaining
>   office easy and smooth for you. But you have made it so that it
>   is difficult, on account of your immense failure and laziness
>   and foolish habits.
>
> 642–7[47]

The key to spotting the connection between Lesbonicus and the Roman *nobilitas* here is Plautus' use of the word *honos* in lines 644 and 646, which has an abstract meaning of "honor" or "esteem," but can also have a more specific meaning of "public office," and indeed, it is the latter meaning that Lysiteles emphasizes here. Lesbonicus' situation seems to resonate with that of the plebeian nobility specifically—his ancestors [*maiores*] and more immediately his father and grandfather [*paterque avosque*] have, through their own hard work and attainment of public office, brought the family into the sphere of the *nobiles*. Now Lesbonicus has the duty to obtain a magistracy of his own [*honorem*] and thus claim the legal right of the same [*honori ... vindex fieres*] for his descendants [*posterorum tuorum*], but instead he is squandering the benefits he inherited and is preventing his descendants from enjoying the same privileges. Whatever Plautus may or may not have been translating from the Greek here, the constellation of words that do appear in the play refer specifically to Roman social classes and political systems. Hölkeskamp explains that it is the attainment of public offices [*honores*] that above all determines an individual's and a family's status among the *nobilitas* at Rome.[48] Furthermore, while an ancestor's previous attainment of the praetorship or consulship might make it easier for his descendants to obtain public office, this did not guarantee continued membership among the *nobiles* if a son or grandson should not live up to the expectations. Hölkeskamp explains: "Even *dignitas*, *gloria* and *auctoritas* inherited from one's forebears had to be permanently and actively reaffirmed and regained ... for the young *nobilis*, this kind of heritage was considered rather a challenge than an asset simply to be taken for granted."[49] This system described by Hölkeskamp is echoed perfectly in Lysiteles' speech.

When these clues about Lesbonicus' identity are collected, it becomes clear that he represents a familiar character for the Romans, a member of the plebeian class, trying to carve out and maintain a place for his family within the Roman aristocracy. Because of the dual system for establishing one's place in Roman society, based on wealth and birth, Lesbonicus is in a uniquely precarious position. While he does enjoy the benefits of wealth and political influence attained by his forebears, he does not have the same all-access pass of a patrician family, the type of family that maps onto Lysiteles and Philto. Through mismanagement of wealth and failure to attain public office, a plebeian family could much more easily return to poverty and obscurity than a patrician family. Even when destitute, patricians were still patricians. To return to Cicero's quote about parallels between Greek-style comedies and Roman realities, it certainly seems that Lesbonicus represents a "carefully fashioned image" of a typical person from Roman "daily life," and the same can also be said of the situation in which Lesbonicus finds himself during the play.

Don't Lose the Farm, Lesbonicus!

After the dowry negotiations between Lysiteles and Lesbonicus break down (711–18), it appears that the family is headed for disaster. While the audience is aware of the hidden treasure and knows of Callicles' real intentions, from the perspective of Lesbonicus and Stasimus, it seems that they are living in a nightmare scenario: the father of the family is abroad, the money has dried up, Lesbonicus has been forced to sell the house for cheap to the man who was supposed to be caring for the family in his father's absence, he is living in a shack on his former property, and now it appears that he will have to sell the farm, the family's last remaining possession, to unscrupulous friends in order to provide a dowry and thus protect his sister in her new marriage. This narrative would have resonated with Plautus' audience as just the kind of thing that was happening to families whose fathers and brothers were away fighting in Rome's citizen armies. The clever tension in *Trinummus* between what *appears* to be happening in the plot and what is *actually* happening is all the more compelling because the threatened outcome for Lesbonicus' family was a real outcome for many members of the audience.

In particular, it is the potential loss of the farm that is so dangerous to Lesbonicus' family. When Lesbonicus insists on using the farm as a dowry, Lysiteles rightly worries that if Lesbonicus gives it away, he will have nothing left with which to reverse his family's slide into destitution [*inopiam*, 652–4; cf., *Inopia* in the prologue]. Lysiteles goes on to say that selling the farm to solve Lesbonicus' money problems will be like putting out the fire on the family hearth, with no spark left to rekindle it (675–8). Even Stasimus, who generally seems to egg his master on in his expenditures, understands the importance of the farm for the survival of Charmides' household. When he first hears Lesbonicus' plan, Stasimus exclaims:

> Master, are you really going to sell off our wet nurse,
> the one who nourishes us? Please, do not do that!
> What are *we* going to eat afterward?
>
> 512–14

While Stasimus' lackluster deception does keep Philto from accepting the farm as dowry (517–61, analyzed in Chapters 2 and 4), Lesbonicus still tries to offer it to Lysiteles in the following scene. The future viability of Charmides' household is balanced on a precipice. For his family to survive, it is imperative that Lesbonicus keep the farm.

The tension in these scenes is easily lost on a modern reader, but the anxiety would have been all too clear to Plautus' contemporaries. While he was writing *Trinummus*, likely during the late 190s BCE, there were middle-class Roman families that found themselves, unexpectedly, in economic distress. These were families who owned moderate tracts of land, some of whom were perhaps even plebeians who, through industry and election to public office, were trying to make their way into the Roman nobility. Husbands, fathers, and brothers were called upon to go abroad with the army to fight against the Seleucid king Antiochus III, in places like Thermopylae and Magnesia. While these men were away, family farms were lost through misuse, mismanagement, or even the misdeeds of patrician neighbors, eager to add to their lucrative estates. What would have been the final straw for some of these families that led them to sell their last remaining tracts of land, thus putting out the fire on their own family hearths and consigning them to the ranks of the urban poor? Perhaps money lost trying to help a friend or the sale of property to provide a dowry for a daughter or a sister? And how would the neighboring aristocrats justify their appropriations, in a world where prosperity was equated with moral goodness? Surely it was the dissolute behavior of the family in question that was the cause, some young man throwing away his father's money on expensive lunches and love affairs. Yes, bad morals were certainly to blame (see Chapter 5), not the capital-hoarding aristocrats racing to the top of Roman society, regardless of who was in the way.

And what would the father of the household say, upon arriving home from war to find his property lost and children in peril? Perhaps it would go something like this:

> **Charmides** Through the most terrible dangers and the deepest seas
>   I have been delivered, through deadly dangers and dens of pirates
>   I saved my own skin. I made it home alive! But now, here,
>   I meet my end, pathetic, all on account of those for whose sake I
>   was forced abroad, at my age.
> The sickness of it steals my breath away.
>
> 1087–91[50]

Such would be a fitting end to a tragedy, but we have not left the world of comedy, as the audience already knows. And so begins an exercise in

Figure 3.1 The return of Charmides, from the 1903 production of *Trinummus* at Westminster School. *The Graphic*, Dec. 19, 1903. Reproduced by kind assistance of the Governing Body of Westminster School.

theatrical wish fulfillment. As it turns out, the farm is still intact, the wealthy neighbor did not cheat the boy but rather purchased the house in order to keep it safe for the father's return. The daughter is engaged to marry into a wealthy family, even if she can't put together a dowry— and let's not forget about the buried treasure hidden inside the house, which ends up safely back in Charmides' hands, not stolen by neighbors or guzzled away by his son, and from which Charmides now provides a dowry for the marriage.[51]

Conclusion

After the initial divine prologue of *Trinummus*, we never again see the characters of Luxuria and Inopia on the stage, though the themes they represent hold our attention throughout. In turn, the inversion in the translation of the play's title from Greek *The Treasure* [*Thensauros*] to Latin *Three Coins/A Day's Wage* [*Trinummus*] draws our attention away from the leisurely wealthy toward the plight of the impoverished. The chilling threat of Destitution [*Inopia*] entering the house of Lesbonicus at the outset is ultimately subverted by the workings of comedy. The anxiety that many in the Roman audience felt daily has been vanquished, albeit temporarily, by the laughter in the theater. But what happens when the festival is over? Would the families of citizen soldiers in Plautus' audience have gone home to find fathers returned safe and sound, plotting neighbors rendered beneficent, advantageous marriages arranged for daughters, and treasure miraculously revealed from within the walls of their own homes? Hardly. Fifty years of further imperial strain on a military and political system designed for a moderately sized city state would lead to the explosion of social distress and violence surrounding Tiberius and Gaius Gracchus, which in turn fueled the fires of civil war that spelled the end of the Republic in the following century. And what was it that was continually at issue in these successive bouts of civil strife? Access to land for the poor, cancelation of debts, an opportunity to escape financial and social oblivion—the same issues that enrich the plot of *Trinummus*. It is illuminating to realize that the social anxieties that undergird the history and literature of the late Republic are also present in the oldest extant corpus of a Roman author, granted we are willing to look for them, rather than point out all the ways Plautus is not Philemon or Menander. When we really look for what is Roman in Roman comedy, we might be surprised at what we find.

4

Religion in *Trinummus*

Introduction: Religion Meets Comedy

(*Various bystanders in the back of the crowd at the Sermon on the Mount*)
"He said, 'Blessed are the cheesemakers.'"
"What's so special about the cheesemakers?"
"Well obviously it's not meant to be taken literally, it refers to any manufacturers of dairy products."

"It's blessed are the meek. Oh, isn't that nice. I'm glad they're getting something because they have a hell of a time."

Monty Python, *Life of Brian*, 1979

In our world, we understand religious parody well enough—e.g., a public screening of Monty Python's *Life of Brian* or a Broadway production of *Book of Mormon: The Musical*. We also have a clear enough conception of a large-scale, public religious celebration—e.g., Easter Mass at the cathedral, Holi at the Krishna temple, etc. But a religious event that contains within it an officially sanctioned opportunity for religious parody—e.g., a screening of *Life of Brian* during Easter Mass—that is more difficult for us to understand, but it is essentially what happened with the performance of comedy at Roman religious festivals.

That is not to say that all religious content in Roman comedy is parodic. There are many references to deities, beliefs, and practices that primarily serve to enrich the curiously hybrid Greco-Roman-ness that is life in Plautinopolis.[1] But since Roman religion focused so much on doing rather than believing, most of the religious material in Plautus can be construed as parody of Roman religious performances. Furthermore, religious parodies in Roman comedy are never just thrown in gratuitously. Whether it is poking fun at the rigidity of Roman prayers (*Cistellaria* 512–27), exploring the connection between morally good behavior and religious observance (*Rudens* prologue), or critiquing the adoption of foreign cults into the Roman religious landscape (*Poenulus*), there is always some sort of important cultural work that religious parody accomplishes in Plautus.[2] For *Trinummus*, the religious material in the text serves primarily to elaborate the theme of class conflict and fair treatment of the poor that we explored in the previous chapter. Before we examine the specific engagements with religious practice in *Trinummus*, we will first look at three important aspects of Roman religion that help explain why religious parody is so prevalent and compelling in these plays.

1) Doing not believing. Since the adoption of Christianity by the Roman emperor Constantine, there has been an emphasis in Western culture on correct belief—orthodoxy—over correct practice—orthopraxy. For example, the Nicene Creed (and the other creeds of early Christianity) delineate proper beliefs about God but say little about proper practices. Prior to this, the emphasis for religions in the Mediterranean region generally was on orthopraxy rather than orthodoxy, as can be seen in a perusal of the Hebrew Bible, especially Leviticus. One result of this is that for the Romans, as long as you were performing the prayers and sacrifices that the gods deemed necessary, you could believe what you wanted about them. What Jupiter and company required was correct performance of the sacrifices and prayers that ensured a harmonious relationship between the gods and the Roman state, a situation the Romans called the "peace of the gods" [*pax deorum*]. Important to this relationship was an idea of reciprocal giving between gods and mortals, a principle expressed in the phrase, "I give so that you may give" [*do ut des*]. Unlike a modern Christian God who may ask for the heart and a willing mind, Roman deities asked for properly sacrificed animals and prayers pronounced with accuracy.[3] When it comes to comedy and parody, the principle of orthopraxy over orthodoxy is important because it can help modern readers understand why such comic license was permitted during the religious festivals. Things that from our perspective may seem sacrilegious were permissible from the Roman perspective, as long as the gods were receiving the offerings they asked for. In fact, the plays themselves, including all the raunchy jokes and religious lampooning, could be considered as offerings to the gods performed before their temples at the religious festivals.

2) Public, not private. One of the hallmarks of modern democratic nations is the separation of church and state. For us, religion is often a private matter. For the Romans, religion was a very public affair and was integrated into practically every aspect of their lives. One large component of this communal religious experience was participation in religious festivals. The Roman calendar was full of annual celebrations for various gods, each with their own rituals and sacrifices. The biggest religious festivals for the Romans were those that had games [*ludi*] associated with them. The games were divided into two main types: *ludi circenses*—chariot races and other events in the Circus Maximus—and *ludi scaenici*—theatrical productions, including Roman comedy. In addition to the sporting and theatrical components, these events also included prayers, sacrifices, and processions with dancing, horseback riding, cult images of the gods, etc. These festivals and the games that accompanied them were an important part of what the gods required from their mortal subjects each year in order to maintain the *pax deorum*.

At the time of Plautus, there were four annual festivals at which plays were performed: the *ludi Megalenses* in April for Magna Mater, a deity imported from Phrygia in 202 BCE, the *ludi Apollinares* in July for Apollo, the *ludi Romani* in September in conjunction with the annual commemoration of Capitoline Jupiter, and the *ludi Plebeii* in November, which mirrored the *ludi Romani* in some respects but were specifically associated with the plebeians, the non-aristocratic faction in the city. Eventually *ludi* were added to the feast of Ceres, the *Cerialia*, in late April, but it is unclear whether this festival included performances during Plautus' day. In addition to these regular events, plays were also performed at triumphal ceremonies, temple dedications, and funerals for the wealthy, each of which fluctuated in their numbers from year to year. C. W. Marshall estimates that there would have been approximately thirty days for performance at Rome each year "and more would not surprise," but this does not include performances at other municipalities, if we image troupes of actors touring around central Italy rather than just operating in Rome.[4] While this number does provide a safe, low-end estimate for performance opportunities, we should think of this as a list of the *known* occasions for performance, not a limit on when performances could have taken place. Amy Richlin rightly questions numbers such as these and suggests that performances of Roman comedy would have been much more prevalent in the city but, given the ephemeral nature of performance, specific data have not survived for much of the performance tradition.[5]

There were no permanent theaters in Rome until the Theater of Pompey was completed in the 50s BCE, which means that during Plautus' day, the city magistrates would set up temporary stages or theaters in varied locations throughout the city, depending on the festival. While there may have been some variation from year to year, it seems that the *ludi plebeii* and *ludi Apollinares* were usually performed in the Circus Flaminius near the Tiber in the Campus Martius, while the *ludi Romani* (and sometimes the *ludi plebeii*) were performed in the Forum, and the *ludi Megalenses* were performed on the Palatine hill, in the plaza in front of the temple of Magna Mater. Frequently, temple steps, store balconies, and other found spaces could be used for seating, which was especially true for the *ludi Megalenses*.[6] We also have records of magistrates commissioning elaborate seating structures and temporary stages, but these come from the late Republic, after Plautus' time.

For modern Western culture, going to the theater is usually a discrete commercial event, not connected with a larger cultural experience like a religious festival. When we consider *Trinummus* (and the rest of Roman comedy for that matter) within this festival context we can see, as the Romans clearly did, that the rituals on which the parodies were modeled were also performed during the festival in close spatial and temporal proximity to the parodies themselves, creating a kind of interperformativity, if you will. Yes, the parodies imitated the language of their models (intertextuality), but the engagement went deeper than this. The parodic prayers and rituals in Plautus included gestures, tableaux, and delivery that reflected the *mise en scène* of their models and were performed in spaces adjacent to those of the religious rituals, if not in the very same space, as would certainly be the case for the *ludi Megalenses*, due to the limited area available in front of the temple of Magna Mater. It is the emphasis on the public and communal aspect of Roman theatrical performance and Roman religious practice that creates this proximity between the parodies and their models.

3) **Polytheistic not monotheistic.** We have already noted how the Roman calendar was full of festivals to various deities. The same polytheistic variety and distribution was mirrored in the urban topography of Rome, with temples, altars, and shrines to a plethora of divine beings interwoven within the plazas, thoroughfares, and alleyways of the city. As Rush Rehm explains, the various rituals of the *ludi* activated "like an electric current, the landscape's potential symbolism."[7] With this in mind, references to certain rituals and prayers to certain deities could take on very different meanings depending on where in the city the play was performed. Proximity to temples would allow actors to gesture toward the gods whom they are addressing. To further enrich this picture, the various temples and shrines throughout the city were built through a unique process that connected them with certain political figures and factions within the city. Roman commanders, at the outset of their campaigns or in the field before battle, would frequently vow to build temples to the deities of their choice using the spoils of their victories, thus endowing these structures with political and ideological meaning, in addition to their religious importance.[8] Because of this, a simple gesture or reference to a temple or cult could carry a whole world of associated meanings along with it. Even though the god mentioned in the text of the play may have had one meaning in

the Greek original on which Plautus based his adaptation, once this was translated into Latin and performed on a Roman stage, it could take on an entirely different range of meanings. Looking for these religious elements in Roman comedy is another excellent way to excavate what is truly Roman from this corpus of plays, rather than trying to reconstruct a Greek original, as we discussed in the previous chapter.

Now, as we turn our attention to the religious material in *Trinummus*, pay attention to how the principles of orthopraxy, public religion, and politically enriched polytheism can help us find additional meaning in the parodic prayers and allusions to ritual feasting and prodigy expiation that we find in the text.

A Dictated Prayer in *Trinummus*

Immediately upon Callicles' entrance in the first scene, we get a reference to domestic Roman religion when Callicles instructs his wife to pray to their household god, the *Lar Familiaris*. This was a particularly Roman practice and so must be a Plautine addition to the Greek material he was adapting. Each Roman household had its own household deities, the *lares* and *penates*, who were seen as responsible for protecting the family line and ensuring that the household flourished in abundance.[9] Callicles addresses his wife as follows:

> **Cal** Wife, I want you to decorate our Lar with a garland
> and pray that this dwelling may turn out
> good, favorable, fruitful, and fortunate for us,
> (*aside*) and that I can see you dead as soon as possible.
>
> 39–42

This brief example illustrates a number of important points about Roman prayer in general and the way Plautus uses prayers in his plays. First of all, the quote does not represent an actual prayer but rather dictated instructions for how to perform one. In Roman ritual, it was imperative that the words and actions of a prayer were performed with extreme accuracy. Any mispronunciation would require the ritual to be started over. Pliny (*HN* 28.11) explains that in public prayers, a priest would dictate the words and actions to a magistrate, with other priests or religious officials standing by to make sure that everything was spoken correctly, and that the audience maintained ritual silence throughout the proceedings. Here we see the hierarchy employed in the state cult mirrored in the domestic sphere, with the husband dictating the words and instructions for the ritual to his wife.

Furthermore, this brief prayer exemplifies the basics of Roman prayer language. Callicles instructs his wife to ask for the gods' favor by using the formula "pray that ..." [*venerare ut* ...]. The use of a verb of petitioning, such as *veneror* or *quaeso*, followed by *ut* and a list of requests is the standard way of formulating a petitionary prayer in Roman religion.[10] The prayer also features a list of synonyms that all describe the desired outcome for the family, namely that the house may turn out "good, favorable, fruitful, and fortunate" [*bona, fausta, felix, fortunata*, 41]. Romans often included repetitive phrases and multiple synonyms in their prayers to ensure that there was no ambiguity in their requests to the gods. This particular example features some nice alliteration in this list as well, which was not ritually required, but could contribute to the overall aesthetics of a prayer. Alliteration like this is a hallmark of both ritual and comic language, as Kathleen McCarthy points out: "The playfulness of farcical language and the solemnity of ritual language in Latin are almost too close for comfort. Both registers rely on alliteration, repetition and pleonasm for their effect."[11]

Up until the final line, the prayer seems entirely cultic—i.e., the kind of thing an actual Roman would say in a genuine ritual—but then Plautus throws in a little joke at the end that provides distance between the stage prayer and an authentic prayer. Here Callicles adds, in a stage whisper, a request that the gods make sure he outlives his wife, a common desire for old men in comedy who are usually depicted at odds with their wives. This pattern of presenting an otherwise cultic prayer with a joke at the end is typical throughout the Plautine corpus.[12] Although these lines of Callicles are brief, they nevertheless exemplify how Plautus engages not only with religious language but also with religious performances. The audience would be very aware of the type of ritual that Callicles is citing—someone in their household likely performed something similar that very morning. Furthermore, the festival at which the play was performed would have featured priests dictating prayers to magistrates in front of a Roman audience. Thus, in this brief prayer at the outset of the play, Plautus provides his audience with a comic echo of rituals that were proximate to the performance of the play.

Feasting with Friends

As we proceed through *Trinummus*, the instances of religious discourse increasingly engage with the theme of social commentary that I outlined in the previous chapter. When Philto is trying to convince Lesbonicus that he should accept the marriage proposal for his sister, he uses a religious feast as an example. Philto imagines a scenario in which Lesbonicus is seated next to a wealthy man at a feast and he asks Lesbonicus whether he would eat from the dishes that the wealthy man's clients bring to him.

Philto describes here a ritual that takes place in or near the temple precinct and includes people from various social classes. It is difficult to pin down which Roman rituals might have featured a feast such as this one. The Romans held public feasts (*cenae populares* as Philto describes them) on various occasions, such as the *ludi Romani*, *ludi plebeii*, and at public funerals organized by wealthy families.[13] At such events, meat from the sacrifices would be supplemented by food purchased by the magistrate in charge, or the family in the case of funerals. The better the feast, the higher the likelihood that the organizer would be chosen for a higher office at the next election.[14] The *ludi Romani* and *plebeii* both featured a special ritual feast called the feast of Jupiter (*epulum Iovis*) at which the senators would feast at public expense near the temples on the Capitoline in the presence of statues of Jupiter, Juno, and Minerva.[15]

These events were strictly segregated by class: only the ruling elite—i.e., those who least needed the aid—held the right to eat at public expense [*ius publice epulandi*].[16]

The two main possibilities for people of different classes to feast together at a public banquet during this period were the Saturnalia and the feast of Hercules at the Ara Maxima.[17] The Saturnalia began on December 17 with a sacrifice at the temple of Saturn, followed by a public feast that anyone was free to attend, while the feast of Hercules on August 12 featured two banquets, the first one early in the day, exclusively for the officiants and senators, and a second, later feast open to all male citizens.[18] These feasts for Hercules were known for the lavish amounts of food provided, all taken from tithes that merchants and politicians dedicated throughout the year, whenever they completed lucrative business deals, celebrated political or military victories, etc.[19] We should also add public funerals to the list of events that allowed feasting across class boundaries, though the frequency and lavishness of such events would vary from year to year. Livy (39.46.2) details one such funeral for P. Licinius Crassus in 184 BCE, the same year as Plautus' death, in which the Forum was filled with tables for feasting and these even had to be covered by awnings because of heavy rains during the event.[20]

Given the strict segregation for most Roman public feasting, there is already something transgressive about Philto's suggestion that members of different social classes might end up on a couch together in the first place.[21] At the heart of this imagined scenario is the question of whether the lower classes should have opportunities to enjoy the same privileges as the upper classes. Lesbonicus thinks the answer is a qualified yes, as long as permission is granted—"I would eat as long as he didn't forbid it," (474), a fitting response for a character who likely represents a plebeian noble trying to maintain a foothold in the world of the elite. Stasimus' response, however, presents a more subversive approach, one that may keep its revolutionary potential hidden beneath the joke for some in the audience. "I would eat, by Pollux," Stasimus proclaims, "even if he forbade it, I would devour with both cheeks full, and that which pleases him, that's what I would seize most of all" (474–5). It is a laugh line, for sure, but there is an edge to it. An enslaved character boldly proclaims to a wealthy elite that he is determined to take what he needs for himself with no regard for the wishes of his "betters." While the crowd in general may have laughed at these silly Greeks allowing a slave to talk this way, some certainly were taking note of the hidden transcript intended for their ears, the radical idea that those on the bottom should also be able to take what they need to live.

Stasimus continues, "I wouldn't yield to him at all, not concerning my life" (477). Roman slaves had no control over their lives. They could be tortured or killed by their masters with impunity, or more commonly, slowly worked to death over long decades of malnourishment and maltreatment. The fact that some slaves at Rome enjoyed privileged status in their households and were eventually able to purchase their freedom should not distract us from the institutional violence at the heart of the system. Stasimus' suggestion of turning the (dinner) tables on the masters forces the audience to contemplate the imbalance of a system in which the wealthy take what they want but it is the poor who are unable to access what they need.

There is also the possibility that Stasimus pushes the social inversion even further by parodying a formula used at the outset of debates in the Roman senate. At lines 478–9, Stasimus says: "It is not fitting for anyone to be modest at the table, for there, decisions are made between the human and the divine" (*verecundari neminem apud mensam decet / nam ibi de divinis atque humanis cernitur*). De Melo identifies this as a reference to a formula used in the senate: "no modesty should dissuade us from speaking our opinions when we debate concerning things human and divine" (*nulla verecundia nos debet demovere a sententia dicunda ubi de rebus divinis et humanis agitur*), though this quote doesn't seem to appear in any classical text.[22] While no evidence can be found that this is an actual senatorial saying from the time of Plautus, the lines are very grand and certainly sound like an official formula. They also provide a somber juxtaposition to the comic image of the slave at the table, elbows out with both cheeks full, and thus work to heighten the humor in this scene.

Stasimus continues the class discourse, proclaiming: "I'll move out of the way for him (i.e., the wealthy man) on the road, or on the foot path, even for public office, but when it comes to my stomach, I'll not budge an inch, by Hercules, unless he beats me down with his fists." It was customary for the lower classes to move out of the way (or be forcibly pushed aside) to allow senators, magistrates, or other powerful and wealthy individuals to pass in the streets.[23] Stasimus seems to appropriate senatorial honors for himself when he says that he, an enslaved person, would kindly step aside for someone like Philto to run for public office, but he holds his ground when it comes to food. Again, this joke covers a hidden message for the poor and hungry: nothing but outright violence will keep Stasimus from claiming sustenance for himself.

More subtle in its subversive outlook is the attitude of Philto in response to Stasimus' interruption. Philto says only two words: *rem fabulare*, "you are speaking to the point," indicating that he agrees with Stasimus' desire to take what he needs from the wealthy. Philto further declares:

> The gods are wealthy, affluence and social status [*factiones*]
> are fitting for them. But for we puny humans . . .
> the indigent [*mendicus*] and the wealthiest [*opulentissumus*], once
>   dead,
> are classified in the same income bracket [*aequo . . . censetur censu*]
> on the shores of the Acheron.
>
> 490–1, 493–4

Philto here uses the same language of class discourse that we analyzed in the previous chapter [*factiones, aequo . . . censetur censu*], and again, he surprisingly uses it to set aside a supposed prerogative, not to assert dominance over his social inferiors. Here is wish fulfillment indeed, a member of the well-fed upper class determined to share his resources with the hungry.[24] Hunger was an inevitable reality for the enslaved and the displaced urban poor in second-century BCE Rome, and Plautus continually refers to hunger as a motivating force throughout his plays, from masters and enslaved foremen who use hunger as a weapon

(*Casina* 126–9; *Mostellaria* 193) to parasites willing to sell family members for a dinner invitation (*Persa* 338).[25]

The awareness that Plautus raises about the plight of hunger should be no less compelling for us today. As of this writing, 42 million people in the US experience food insecurity (1 in 8 adults), including 13 million children (1 in 6).[26] For the collection of fifty-two countries designated as the Europe and Central Asia group, the UN reports: "111 million people (11.9 percent of the total population) were moderately or severely food insecure in 2020," an increase of more than 14 million people in one year, largely due to the Covid outbreak.[27] The catalogue of such statistics, sadly, could go on and on—these are just two examples. Pandemics come and go, but the plague of hunger has been a constant curse for humanity.

At the end of this section, Stasimus returns to the theme of religion by explaining, "with the cost of food so high, a dinner is an inheritance without sacrifices" (*cena hoc annona est sine sacris hereditas*, 484), referring to the Roman custom of inheritances that were granted with the stipulation that the heir would offer regular sacrifices on behalf of the deceased.[28] Throughout this scene, Plautus cites religious practices pertaining to feasting and sacrifices that may have been on display during the very festival at which the play was performed. The impact of the scene would have been increased if the play were performed at the *ludi Romani* or *ludi plebeii*, during which the feasting at the *epulum Iovis* was highly segregated and exclusive. Thus, Plautus addresses the disparities between the wealthy and poor in Rome, illustrating how religious customs usually reinforced inequality rather than alleviated it. With the deck stacked against the urban poor, it's up to individuals to take the initiative to share their privileges with the less fortunate, as Philto tries to do in this scene.

Prodigies at the Farm

Later on in this same scene, Stasimus again appropriates the prerogatives of the Roman elite when he uses the language of prodigies and expiation to dissuade Philto from accepting the farm as a dowry. Romans were always on the lookout for odd or frightening occurrences that could be understood as signs that the peace between mortals and gods (*pax deorum*) was in danger. Such phenomena could include unusual weather, especially lightning strikes in significant places, abnormal animal births and behavior, and fire, sweat, or voices seeming to come from statues of the gods, etc. The Romans referred to these occurrences as prodigies, and one important religious role of the senate was to collect reports of prodigies and decide which ones were serious enough to require expiatory sacrifices. At least once per year, more frequently if something extreme were observed, the senate would send a list of actionable prodigies to a college of priests known at Plautus' time as the *decemviri sacris faciundis*, a panel of ten men who consulted the books of the Sibylline oracles and decided what expiatory actions needed to be taken to repair the breach in the *pax deorum*.

In Chapter 2, we briefly discussed Stasimus' lackluster deception scene, in which he convinces Philto not to accept Lesbonicus' farm as a dowry. In the context of stock characters, the scene is significant because it is underwhelming in its creativity and effect on the action of the play, but in the context of religion, there are interesting connections to Roman practices regarding prodigies. On one level, Stasimus just describes a farm that is comically unprofitable for the owner. But, when we remember the religious frame of Plautine drama, we can see that many of the troubles at the farm that Stasimus describes could be considered prodigies. Stasimus repeatedly describes anomalous animal behavior, including sudden death and abnormal appearance. Oxen die repeatedly while plowing (523–4), pigs die of acute sickness (540), and sheep fail to produce wool (541). Death of those working on the farm is even extended to the human sphere as well. Stasimus says that, of the enslaved laborers, even the hardiest last only six months (542–4) and that many of the former owners either died randomly or killed themselves, though some ran off into exile instead (535–6). There are repeated crop failures on the farm. Grapes hang rotten on the vine before they ripen (526) and the owners usually get three times less grain than they plant, even when the crop is abundant everywhere else (529–30). And the most significant prodigy of all: every other tree on the property has been struck by lightning (539). Stasimus attributes all of this to the fact that there is a portal to the underworld on the farm, as he nonchalantly claims in the middle of his litany of disasters (525).

Some of these things might not count as prodigies on their own, but when they are all concentrated on one locale, the connection becomes clear. Stasimus here engages in the religious discourse of the elite, providing a list of prodigies to Philto, who, for his part, is convinced by Stasimus' warning and claims that the farm will never become his (559). This moment is comparable to the scene in *Mostellaria*, when the clever slave Tranio uses the religious beliefs of the old man Theopropides to frighten him away from entering his own house (431–531). Thus, Stasimus manipulates language and imagery regarding prodigies, normally the purview of the Roman elite, in order deceive Philto.

A Prayer to Neptune

The combination of religious language and class discourse is further explored in the prayer to Neptune that Charmides offers when he arrives home from his travels. At the outset, the prayer adheres to the pattern of cultic language followed by jokes that we saw earlier in the prayer that Callicles dictated to his wife (39–42). Here is what Charmides says in this scene:

> To you Neptune, ruler of the salt sea, ruler of many, brother of celestial Jove,[29]
> pleasantly with pleasure my praises I offer you and gratefully I give gratitude also
> to the salty waves,
> in whose power I was repeatedly placed, as to what would become of my goods
> and my life.

> Since they returned me safely from their realm, all the way back to my ancestral
> city, I give thanks.
> And I to you, Neptune, before all the other gods, give and direct the greatest
> thanks,
> for everyone says that you are savage, uncivilized, and greedy to boot,
> a smutty, monstrous, insufferable madman—but by experience I found you to be
> the opposite.
> Yes, by Pollux, while at sea I found you to be peaceful and kind, much to my
> liking, just as I wanted.
>
> 820–7

The prayer opens with a long invocation that delineates the powers of Neptune and his relationship to Jupiter, followed by a clause of thanksgiving that is filled with alliteration and pleonasm, all typical elements of Roman prayer language (*laetus lubens laudis ago et gratis gratiasque habeo*, 821). Charmides then states the reason for his gratitude, namely his safe arrival home. In fact, in line 823 he uses language similar to prayers of thanksgiving offered by victorious generals at their arrival home, an element that could bolster the allusions to military service in Charmides' character that I argued for in the previous chapter.[30] Everything seems to follow standard Roman prayer language, until we get to line 825, where Charmides names all the bad things people say about Neptune, but then claims that he disagrees.[31] This line is humorous in itself, but it gets even funnier when the list carries over into the next line, with the adjectives "smutty, monstrous, insufferable, insane" [*spurcificum, immanem, intolerandum, vesanum*]—these words definitely do not appear in a typical prayer! Charmides, however, smooths it all over by saying that he disagrees with the common assessment.

As the prayer continues, Charmides returns to the theme of social classes, using the word *ordo*, another echo to the discussion of social classes between Philto and Lesbonicus from Chapter 3. In this scene, Charmides continues his prayer thus:

> atque hanc tuam gloriam iam ante auribus acceperam, et nobilest
>   apud homines,
> pauperibus te parcere solitum, dites damnare atque domare.
> abi, laudo, scis ordine, ut aequomst, tractare homines. hoc dis
>   dignumst;
> semper mendicis modesti sint.

> With my ears I had already previously heard this reputation, and it is
>   well known among men,
> that you are accustomed to spare the poor and censure and subdue
>   the wealthy.
> Go, then, I praise you. You know how to treat men according to their
>   status, as is fair.
> This is worthy of the gods—may they always be kind to the poor.
>
> 828–31[32]

On first appearance, it seems that Charmides here is praising Neptune for his attention to the poor, but there is disagreement among editors regarding these lines, with the majority actually construing line 830, "you know how to treat men according to their status," as a rejection of the idea that the gods would favor the poor over the wealthy. In fact, most editors put square brackets around the phrase "may they always be kind to the poor" [*semper mendicis modesti sint*], indicating that they believe the line should be removed from the play. The reasons for the removal are more ideological than philological. I have decided to keep the line because it reflects the status of Charmides' family as a household in economic peril, as elaborated in Chapter 3. For those interested in observing philology in action, I provide additional details on this controversy in Appendix B.

If we keep line 831, the support for the poor in the audience seems quite overwhelming, but Plautus designed the preceding line with purposeful ambiguity so as not to criticize the wealthy too forcefully, since this was not a game without consequences, as we see from the anecdote of Naevius' imprisonment for criticizing the Metelli onstage.[33] Here it is the use of the word "go" [*abi*] in line 830 that brings in the ambiguity. Literally, this word means "depart" or "go away" but it is used colloquially in Latin as either a mild reproach or, in the exact opposite sense, as a sign of approval. Compare the phrase "get out of here," in English, which could show up between friends as "Get out of here! You did so great on that exam!" or between enemies as "Get out of here!" accompanied by smashing dishes and a slamming door. Gray construes *abi* as a mild reproach, indicating rejection of the claim of the previous line that Neptune helps the poor. Wagner, on the other hand, takes *abi* as an expression of "praise and approbation" that flows naturally into line 831, "may they always be kind to the poor."[34] When we consider this ambiguity, it is clear to see that Gray is just seeing these lines the way the Roman elite would have seen them. However, when we take up the perspective of the free urban poor and the enslaved, as Richlin (2017) suggests, there is a powerful feeling of wish fulfillment in the idea that the gods would aid those who need it most, but this message was likely lost on the elite. Besides, the whole point of hidden transcripts shared among subalterns is that they are hidden from those in power. Ambiguity and plausible deniability are the watchword for a poet who wants to critique power structures but still stay in business. And we cannot forget how important the actor's delivery could be in tipping the scale one way or the other.

Since we are now on the topic of performance, we can ask whether there was anything about the performance context that could have further inflected the audience's understanding of this prayer. While there is no indication of exactly where and when this play was performed originally, let's posit a performance in the Circus Flaminius, an oblong plaza in the Campus Martius near the Tiber and a common location for the Plebeian Games [*ludi plebeii*] and the Games of Apollo [*ludi Apollinares*]. On the northern side of the Circus Flaminius, near the center of the plaza, there was a temple of Neptune.[35] While there is no direct evidence that Neptune was associated with the plebeian class at

Rome in the same way that, say, Ceres was, the location itself may have created an implied connection. The legal assemblies of the plebeians [*concilium plebis*] took place in the Circus Flaminius and, as previously mentioned, this was the location of the annual Plebeian Games.[36] Neptune doesn't appear often on Roman coinage, but one noteworthy example comes from a coin minted in 60 BCE by P. Plautius Hypsaeus, a prominent member of the plebeian nobility.[37] Furthermore, rowing in the navy, an activity inherently connected with Neptune, was a task associated with the lowest property classes because no special military equipment like a horse or armor was necessary. In addition to the evidence from the text, the image of Neptune as a god who favors the poor would be emphasized all the more in performance if the play were presented at the Plebeian Games, in the very location where the plebeian assembly met, with the temporary theater in sight of the temple of Neptune, allowing the actor to gesture toward it during his prayer.

Conclusion: Jupiter as Landowner

In his vivid descriptions of his alleged travels, the conman tells Charmides that he journeyed all the way to the headwaters of the river that pours from beneath Jupiter's throne, paddling upstream in a fishing smack. When a snarky Charmides asks if he got to see Jupiter himself, the conman responds, without missing a beat, "The other gods said he went to his country estate to distribute rations to his slaves" (939–44). Even in this brief joke we see the idea that the divine sphere mirrors the social stratification of the human sphere, but at least Jupiter is a benevolent master: he goes personally to provide food for the slaves at his latifundia, a reprise of the benevolent god from Charmides' prayer who helps the poor, mixed with the wealthy man at the feast who allows his social inferiors to eat at his table. The wish that those with resources to share might help the indigent, here expressed through religious language and imagery, is juxtaposed with the lament of the conman before he begins his scam, "Do you see what sort of bad business poverty provides to a destitute man, what I am forced to do for just three coins?" (847–8), a lament that certainly has a metatheatrical bite to it, as the impoverished or even enslaved actor stands in front of the elites in the front rows, singing for his supper.

Religious performances at Rome were both highly visible and highly segregated along class lines. In *Trinummus*, we see how Plautus uses echoes of and allusions to religious practices to enrich the social commentary of the play and to weave the dramatic performance into the larger context of the religious festival. Through his clever use of humor and ambiguity, Plautus packages these messages within a comedy full of laughs at the surface level, but with weightier messages for those willing to wade in deeper.

5

A Moral Play or a Play on Morals?

Introduction

Gripus: I have seen comic actors sagely pronounce sayings like this,
and get applause for them, when they demonstrate wise morals to the
  people,
but when the crowd splits up and each goes to their own home,
no one acts how those actors told them to. *Rudens* 1249–53

Before you criticize someone, you should walk a mile their shoes.
That way, when you criticize them, you are a mile away from them . . .
  and you have their shoes. Anonymous[1]

Up to this point, we have discussed some genuinely funny aspects of *Trinummus*, like the characters imitating each other's stock types throughout, scenes of comic miscommunication, and some laughworthy religious parodies. Despite these humorous aspects, scholarly appraisals of the play and opportunities for modern performances have been tied not to the humor of the play, but to its moral sentiments, and to be fair, there are a lot of moral sentiments in the play. Four major scenes deal directly with the theme of public morality, and when these are combined with a list of one- or two-line moral maxims expressed by characters in the play, roughly one third of the dialogue can be classified as moralizing in some respect.[2] The mere saturation of the moralizing content in the play should, however, lead us to question how seriously we are to take Plautus' moral messaging in *Trinummus*. When the volume is turned up so loud, do these moments come across as more satirical than sincere? In this chapter, we will explore this question by first delving into the performance history of the play, with specific focus on a series of productions of *Trinummus* at Westminster School in London from 1860 to 1903. This case study is particularly pertinent here, since *Trinummus* was chosen for these performances on account of it being a morally appropriate play for teenagers to perform. Despite the "profound wisdom which breathes though every scene of the comedy," as one reviewer describes it, after more than forty years of experimentation with *Trinummus* as a vessel for moral education, the play was ultimately replaced in the annual cycle of Westminster School productions by a bowdlerized version of Terence's *Eunuchus*.[3] The answer to why the *Trinummus* was abandoned may lie in the structure of the play itself. When the one-liners and soliloquies are taken out of context, they can sound like the very thing that bright young minds ought to hear when preparing to embark on a career of politics and public service. However, when we explore the moral *sententiae* and speeches from *Trinummus* in context, we can identify a number of factors that suggest satire rather than sincerity.

In the second half of the chapter, we will examine the moral *sententiae* and monologues of *Trinummus* and observe how the context frequently undercuts the moral messages of the characters, from the self-righteous Megaronides, who falls victim to the very unfounded gossip that he decries, to the inebriated preaching of the penitently truant (rather than truly penitent) Stasimus, who has recently been robbed by his rowdy drinking buddies. Ultimately, it is up to Plautus' readers, viewers, and performers to decide whether Plautus, in his old age, has thrown his lot in with the moralists or whether he just repeats their moral posturing back at them through characters who are incongruent with the ethical messages they declaim and who fail to live up to the morals they preach.

Trinummus at Westminster School

When we examine the performance history of *Trinummus*, the archival material available is less robust than for some of Plautus' better-known plays, like *Miles* or *Pseudolus*.[4] The earliest documented performances of *Trinummus* took place in Renaissance Italy (Ferrara 1499, Mantua 1502 and 1525), with additional productions staged in Cambridge 1563 and Munich 1566.[5] Despite this early humanist interest, the play drops off the radar until the mid-1800s, when it became a regular choice for performance at schools and universities. The aforementioned productions at Westminster School in London led the way, beginning in 1860, followed by a few productions at Radley College in Oxfordshire in the 1880s and 90s.[6] Across the Atlantic, as colleges and universities were experimenting with performances in Greek and Latin, *Trinummus* was included among the Roman plays selected, with productions at Syracuse University (1895), Smith College (1900), Swarthmore College (1902), Amherst College (1904), Earlham College (1909), the University of Nebraska (1910), and Washburn College (1910).[7] After this cluster of productions in the late nineteenth and early twentieth centuries, interest in *Trinummus* again waned, with the only other documented performances in 1959 as a BBC radio drama, in 2000 as part of a theater festival at Ancient Elea, Italy, and most recently in 2019 at the City Theater of Locri, Italy.[8]

From this performance history, I have chosen the series of ten productions at Westminster School from 1860 to 1903 to serve as a case study, due to the school's extended engagement with the play and their excellent documentation of the performances.[9] As can be seen by scanning the dates (1860, 1865, 1869, 1874, 1879, 1883, 1888, 1893, 1897, and 1903), the productions at Westminster marked the beginning of the renewed interest in *Trinummus* for its educational potential during the 1800s. The performance of ancient drama at Westminster School, also known as St. Peter's College, dates back to 1560, when Queen Elizabeth stipulated in the school's charter that the young men at the school should present a play in Latin during the Christmas season, in order to better enjoy the holidays [*majori cum frutu tempus Natalis terat*], but more importantly, so that the pupils could develop their skills at public speaking by learning proper action and pronunciation [*tum actioni tum pronunciationi decenti melius se assuescat*].[10] The first performances

Figure 5.1 Painting of a performance at Westminster School. F. Fenton, 1897. Reproduced by kind assistance of the Governing Body of Westminster School.

took place in 1563, with productions of Terence's *Heautontimoroumenos* [*Self-Tormentor*] and Plautus' *Miles Gloriosus* [*Braggart Soldier*].[11] By 1704, a cycle of four plays was established, including *Amphitruo* by Plautus and Terence's *Eunuchus*, *Phormio*, and *Adelphi*, with one play performed each year, except when interrupted by war or high-level state funerals. Shortly after the cycle was started, *Amphitruo* was replaced by *Andria* in 1711, so that Terence dominated the selection until 1860 when *Trinummus* was chosen to replace *Eunuchus*.[12]

Each year when the plays were presented, the performances were framed by prologues and epilogues composed in Latin. While the prologues tended to be more serious in nature, consisting mainly of reminders about the longevity of the performance tradition, notices of important events for the year, obituaries of former Westminster graduates, etc., the epilogues, on the other hand, were novel dramatic compositions written in elegiac couplets that engaged with the themes of the play but placed the characters in farcical contemporary situations with jokes based heavily on current events. The ever-hungry parasites Phormio (*Phormio*) and Gnatho (*Eunuchus*) get to feast in London restaurants while enslaved characters, like Davos (*Andria*) and Parmeno (*Eunuchus*), gain freedom and set up shop as respectable tradesmen, or perhaps just engage in some Victorian-style street boxing.[13] For *Trinummus* specifically, the epilogues portray the various characters running a boarding school (1869), excavating for the underground railroad (1874), discovering antiquities at Pompeii and Troy (1879), returning from the Klondike (1897), and setting off for an excursion to the Chicago World's Fair (1893), not to mention a rousing game of cricket and more than one visit by Busby, the resident ghost of the Westminster dormitories.[14] Despite the far-fetched scenarios, the epilogues are full of echoes to the action of the play—the sale of the house and the need to find and preserve the treasure are frequently important, as are attempts by Stasimus and the conman to deceive the

Figure 5.2 Lesbonicus as a cricketer from the 1897 epilogue. *The Illustrated Sporting and Dramatic News*, Jan. 1, 1898. Reproduced by kind assistance of the Governing Body of Westminster School.

Figure 5.3 Rats escaping from the inn run by Lesbonicus and Stasimus; Charmides returning from the Klondyke, and the Sycophant dressed as a Turk, from the 1897 epilogue. *The Illustrated Sporting and Dramatic News*, Jan. 1, 1898. Reproduced by kind assistance of the Governing Body of Westminster School.

old men in some respect. Even the play's preoccupation with economic issues filters through into these afterpieces, as seen in discussions about employment for the poor and the happenings at the stock exchange. When we take into account the fanciful epilogues of the plays, it is apparent that these annual productions at Westminster constituted not only revivals of the original Latin play but also adaptations of *Trinummus* that juxtapose the themes and characters with contemporary concerns.

As noted, *Trinummus* wasn't initially part of the four-year cycle of plays at the school. Until 1860, the slot had been held by Terence's *Eunuchus*, but pressure from those wishing to end the tradition of Latin plays on moral grounds, combined with a transition to a new headmaster in 1855, led to a change in the rotation.[15] A central scene of *Eunuchus* features a young man who disguises himself as a eunuch so he can infiltrate the house of a prostitute and rape a woman whom he has been stalking. Many ancient comedies include sexual assault in the backstory of the plot, but *Eunuchus* is unique in that the assault is perpetrated by one of the main characters during the course of the play, albeit offstage.

Given this bit of information, it is perhaps more remarkable that *Eunuchus* was chosen at all for performance at Westminster than that it was eventually replaced by *Trinummus*.[16] By the 1770s, the scene in which the false eunuch reports his actions to his friend had been removed from the performance script, but debate continued over whether such plays should be performed at all at the school, eventually coming to a head in 1847 when Dean Buckland announced that he would put an end to the annual performances, despite their inclusion in the original charter of the school. This proposal met with stiff resistance from Westminster graduates who now filled some of the highest positions in the country, including Prime Minister John Russell, and Thomas Musgrave, the Archbishop of York.[17] When *Trinummus* was chosen to replace *Eunuchus* in 1860, it was seen as an answer to this ongoing debate, a way to keep the tradition alive by performing an ancient Latin play, but one full of moral sentiment and devoid of any offensive calories—like drinking a diet soda.[18]

Trinummus, then, a play which, according to one reviewer, "had not been acted within the practical memory of man," was adopted specifically because it was seen as a compromise between the Westminster traditionalists and the moral reformers.[19] But did the compromise work? Well, it depends on whom you ask. During the ten-production run, from 1860 to 1903, opinions were split. After the first performance in 1860, the writer for the *Daily Telegraph* gushes, "Next to the *Captivi*, the *Trinummus* is Plautus' best composition in respect to its admirable design, the delineation of character shown in it, and the skilful arrangement of the parts," even claiming of Lysiteles that "a more finished and beautifully consistent character it would be impossible to find." Remember, this is the same character that a century later Anderson would describe as an "insufferable prig" who "dwindles into a self-righteous pompous ass," which is evidence of just how much tastes change over time when it comes to comedy and moralizing.[20] But, in 1860, the adoption of *Trinummus* for the Westminster stage was hailed as a moral victory that delivered a play not at all inferior to the *Eunuchus*. "Yet see in this *Trinummus* how happily drawn are the pictures, how

Figure 5.4 Lysiteles argues with Lesbonicus while Stasimus watches. *Illustrated London News*, Dec. 25, 1869. Courtesy of the Archive of Performances of Greek and Roman Drama, Oxford.

various the incidents, how meritorious the dialogues, how natural the conclusion! There is life before you—there is sharp, sprightly raillery—there is a bustle—there is surprise—there are all sorts of unexpected situations!"[21]

While the initial reviews in 1860 were positive, in subsequent years, reviewers were less enthusiastic about the change from *Eunuchus* to *Trinummus*. As the writer for the *Graphic* explains after the 1869 production, "It is questionable whether the reformation was wisely effected. *Trinummus* is an exceedingly dull play, in spite of its unquestionable moral tendency, and very inadequately represents the genius of Plautus ... There is a heaviness in *Trinummus* which, in spite of a broadly farcical scene [i.e. the scene with the conman], nothing can overcome."[22] Later, in 1883, the writer for the *Saturday Review* states:

> No doubt this play was chosen in preference to others by the same author on account of its freedom from anything which could offend

against modern ideas of decency. Necessary as such considerations are, the choice is in some respects to be regretted. The *Trinummus* gives comparatively little idea of the chief characteristics of Plautus as contrasted with Terence. In scarcely any of his comedies do we find so little of the exuberant vigour and the intense love of fun for its own sake which distinguish him from his more refined successor.[23]

As these quotes illustrate, reviewers did not deny that *Trinummus* was morally preferable to *Eunuchus* and that it was chosen for performance at the school on these grounds, but they also agree that *Trinummus* is an inadequate representative of Plautine drama as whole. The reason they felt this way ties in with ideas that we explored in Chapter 2—the humor in *Trinummus* is best seen when it is considered alongside other Roman comedies in which the characters behave in a more expected fashion. As a stand-alone sample of Plautine dramaturgy, the humor that stems from the unexpected behavior of the characters in *Trinummus* can fall flat. Maurice Davies certainly sums up the feelings of many in the audience at these Westminster productions of *Trinummus* (though the same could be said of many high school plays, sans the quip about the quality of the Latin, of course): "We grin and bear it, lost in amazement at the prodigious sacrifice made by the young dramatis personae for our delectation in committing to memory twelve hundred lines of colloquial and rather unrhythmical Latin."[24]

Even though the reviews overall trend from positive to negative over time, there were still fans of *Trinummus* all the way to the end of its time at Westminster. In fact, some of the most ebullient praise is to be found in the reviews of the 1897 production. The writer for the *Standard* boldly proclaims that *Trinummus* is "the noblest of the plays which bear the name of Plautus and one of the very finest comedies in Latin literature," even going on to claim (without irony, I may add) that Lysiteles' soliloquy "might have been put in the mouth of Hamlet," and that the scene with the conman is so good that "nothing sharper, keener, or more full of the true comic spirit was ever composed by Molière."[25] While such statements may indicate that the reviewer has not actually read much Shakespeare or Molière, it is instructive to note that these (too) high opinions of the play were again directly linked to its moral content. The same reviewer says that *Trinummus* is "the greatest comedy ... not for its dramatic representation of human nature, but for what the Germans would call its ethical contents." For now, we'll skip over the ethnocentric shade thrown at the pioneers of *Altertumswissenschaft*, and follow up the author's emphasis on the ethical contents of the play with the reviewer's opinions about the moral sententiae expressed by the old men in *Trinummus*:

> They all see with grief and dread the deterioration of public and private morals which had set in, and cling tenaciously to the golden age of manners and civic virtue which new tastes and habits were rapidly breaking down ... From their mouths throughout the whole play there fall in the richest abundance precepts of individual morality and duty, and reflections relating to public conduct, which certainly express the highest ethics of the pre-Christian Pagan world.

These quotes make it clear that in the 1890s, *Trinummus* was still being celebrated as a moral success. It is curious, then, that the 1893 performance at Westminster saw the introduction of an abridged script of the play that cut over one third of the lines (from 1,189 to 759) and greatly reduced the moralizing content.[26] A collation of the 1893 abridgment with Lindsay's Oxford text reveals that, of the 430 lines removed, nearly half (192) contain moralizing content of some sort. Included among the scenes left on the cutting-room floor are Megaronides' initial monologue that sets up the theme of morality for the play (28–38), Lysiteles' entire song about love vs industry (223–75), many of the sententiae exchanged between Lysiteles and Philto (small cuts here and there from 276 to 399), and Lysiteles' speech to Lesbonicus about honoring the work of his ancestors, along with Lesbonicus' snarky responses (641–78). Furthermore, most of the cuts come from the first two thirds of the play, which draws the audience's attention away from the discussions about the dowry and proper behavior for young men and toward the deception scene between Charmides and the conman—only four lines are removed from this latter scene.

These cuts did not go without notice by those familiar with their Plautus. The same enthusiastic reviewer of the 1897 production remarks: "But [*Trinummus*] has been sadly mauled about in cutting it down. Scenes of great pith and moment in the development of such character as the piece exhibits, and lines of great interest for the complete understanding of a situation have been taken out by some condenser who has not quite risen to the level of his work."[27] When the goal of substituting *Trinummus* for *Eunuchus* was to emphasize the moral instruction of the pupils at the school, why would such a large quantity of the moral statements be removed from the performance script? I maintain that one of the things that makes the moralizing content of the play feel like parody is the sheer quantity of the moralizing speeches and *sententiae*. When you reduce that number, it is easier to take the balance as sincere. Whatever the rationale, by 1907 the experiment of swapping the plays was deemed unsuccessful and *Trinummus* was ousted from the regular cycle by an adaptation of *Eunuchus* titled the *Famulus* (*Footman*) in which the young man who perpetrates the sexual assault in Terence's original instead dresses up as a servant and, after infiltrating the house of a respectable widow (not a prostitute), only gawks awkwardly at his love interest, the widow's young ward, before escaping to announce his exploits.[28] By 1907, *Trinummus* couldn't compete with a century-and-a-half tradition of Terence over Plautus at the school and, in the end, what was seen as Plautus' moralizing snoozer was replaced by a (dare we say) neutered *Eunuchus*.[29]

This case study demonstrates how the performance history of *Trinummus* has been tied to the reception of the moralizing content of the play. If the parodic exuberance of the moral *sententiae* failed to come through in the performances at Westminster School, the play's potential for social and economic commentary was heard loud and clear, especially in the playful epilogues that were composed in response to Plautus' text.

Surprisingly for an all-boys school, the lack of female characters in the text was noticed and remedied in a number of the epilogues, such as

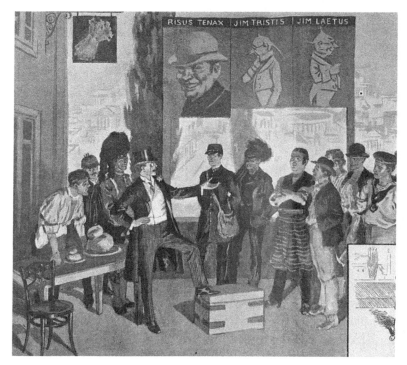

Figure 5.5 Characters showing class divides in the 1903 epilogue. *The Graphic*, Dec. 19, 1903. Reproduced by kind assistance of the Governing Body of Westminster School.

the 1869 epilogue, in which Lesbonicus' sister is depicted alongside her brother as a teacher at a private school, advocating for instruction in "modern" science and women's rights. This all seems like a step forward, until we read that her husband Lysiteles is described as "hen-pecked" and "under a harsh dominion" [*pexus-gallinae, dura sub ditione*], while her teachings are upstaged by her grumbling father-in-law Philto, whose remarks are at least "gallantly modified so as not to graze the feelings of the ladies who patronize the performance."[30]

In 1883, the epilogue turned from gender roles to economic and class concerns. The scene opens outside a pub with a chorus of laborers, shovels in hand, who are soon joined by Stasimus, now a soldier

A Moral Play or a Play on Morals?

Figure 5.6 Men and women in the audience sitting separately at the 1869 production, with the prologue speaker depicted between the two groups. *The Graphic*, Dec. 25, 1869. Reproduced by kind assistance of the Governing Body of Westminster School.

returning from Egypt ("I like the art of war—but not the filthy folk of the Nile," he proclaims),[31] and their former master Callicles, a country gentlemen who has been forced by hard times to pick up a shovel, this time not to dig up a treasure, but to join the laborers. The discussion of what to do under economic distress is soon upstaged by the entrance of Lysiteles and Lesbonicus, two university students, who are in the throes of a furious debate about the relative merits of Cambridge and Oxford. When they realize they are being observed by a chorus of workmen, Lesbonicus suggests that art will solve all their problems and make their labor sweet (*arte labor dulcis*), promising that work fields will give way to pleasure gardens, and there will be perpetual spring and peace (*cedant arva hortis tandem ... perpetuo vere, quiesque siet*). While this appeals to some of the laborers ("Spring is nice," one says—*ver placet*), others ask more practical questions about wages and food (*Ubi merces nostra? Cibusque?*), to which Lesbonicus replies, "Let the violets, lilies, myrtles, and waters provide. Then virtue

Figure 5.7 Lady's Ticket with wax seal and handwritten date and time for the 1874 production. Reproduced by kind assistance of the Governing Body of Westminster School.

will be your wages." After these sentiments are laughed down by the crowd, the more practical Lysiteles suggest that the men be put to work dredging the Cam River, while Philto and Charmides propose building a shipping canal or a tunnel across the English Channel. While the subject matter is clearly connected to London in the 1880s, the dynamic of social classes at odds with each other is maintained from Plautus' original.

For the epilogue in 1893, Megaronides, Callicles, and Philto each represent gentlemen from the various political factions, who sit on a bench and buy newspapers from the news vendor Stasimus. While they disagree about various matters of legislation and policy (Callicles refers to Megaronides' grumpy rejoinder about the Newcastle Programme of 1891 as "sour grapes"—*acerba est uva!*),[32] their secure status in society allows them to sit back and comment on the actions of those fighting for equality. The composers of the epilogue take Plautus' prologue characters Luxuria and Inopia and transform them into contemporary London women. Luxuria ends up as Lesbonicus' overbearing wife, a nod to the comment in Plautus' text that Lesboncius lost the family wealth with Luxuria as his accomplice (13). Lesbonicus enters in a flurry, chased by Luxuria who is determined to "get her rights" from him (*Pol, posco mea iura!* —"By Pollux, I'm seeking my rights!"), as she decries Lesbonicus' audacity in thinking that he is her equal (*seque mihi postulat esse parem*—"and he suggests that he is equal to me").[33] The situation

THE WESTMINSTER PLAY: SCENE FROM THE EPILOGUE. INOPIA ADDRESSING THE UNEMPLOYED IN TRAFALGAR SQUARE

Figure 5.8 Inopia addresses the unemployed in the 1893 epilogue. *The Graphic*, Dec. 23, 1893. Reproduced by kind assistance of the Governing Body of Westminster School.

itself is already a travesty of women's rights and the suffrage movement, but Megaronides makes the character of Luxuria seem even more ridiculous by remarking to the audience that if she stood on her head, she would look like a mushroom (*Pol hanc, in vertice si stet, Fungini generis iure voces specimen*). This is certainly a reference to the exaggerated skirt that the male actor wore in his portrayal Luxuria, but it is also a clever nod to the quip that Charmides makes about the conman's hat in the original text of the play (851).[34] Just as we saw in our analysis of Plautus' text in Chapter 2, the ability to deliver asides increases a character's rapport with the audience while at the same time undermining the position of the characters who do not acknowledge the aside.[35] With this in mind, we can see how the text of the epilogue undermines characters who present socially progressive ideas by utilizing some of Plautus' original dramatic techniques, namely humorous costumes and asides.

The same tactic of building rapport through asides is used when Inopia comes onstage leading a crowd of unemployed coal miners. Philto remarks, "Am I deceived, or are the streets besieged by raging commoners?" (*Fallor? an obsessae plebe furente viae*).[36] Inopia, who has become a coal miner's wife, stands on a stool and cries out:

> Mi auferte tyrannos! . . .
> O cives, cives, quaerenda pecunia primum!
> Num sinitis miseros interiisse fame?

> Bring the tyrants out to me!
> O citizens, citizens, wages must be sought first!
> Will you really allow the wretched to die from hunger?

Lesbonicus, who also turns out to be an unemployed miner, joins in with Inopia, while Philto and Callicles, secure in their wealth, make wry comments from the sidelines:

> **Lesb** Nos domini excludunt saevi, sociata caterva;
>
> Queis vivi possit praemia danda negant.
>
> **Inop** Euge! πάλιν! **Lesb:** Fodere e terra possumque voloque—

Phil (*aside*). Sed mendicari non pudet.

Cal (*aside*). Euge! πάλιν!

Lesb Our savage masters shut us out, my crowd of comrades,

We to whom they say that it is not possible to pay a living wage!

Inop Bravo! Again! **Lesb:** I am capable of digging in the ground and I want to—

Phil (*aside*). But he's not ashamed to go begging.

Cal (*aside*). Bravo! Again!

Here again, those secure in their social position use their ability to deliver asides to the audience in order to undermine the marginalized in their search for equality, this time in the form of living wages for coal miners, a discussion not so different from those happening now in the US concerning a new federal minimum wage.[37] In our scene from 1893, the burgeoning riot is derailed when the Sycophant arrives and offers to conduct everyone off to Chicago to see the World's Fair, but then secretly absconds with the collected funds and heads for Argentina. Things could have been worse, I suppose—when Lesbonicus asks who the leader of the expedition should be, Megaronides exclaims, "Just don't let it be a woman!" [*modo ne sit femina!*].[38]

These samples from the Westminster play epilogues show us that commentary on social inequality is encoded in the DNA of Plautus' *Trinummus*. If we consider this through the lens of Linda Hutcheon's work on adaptation, we can see that the writers of the epilogues, in adapting the text of *Trinummus*, used the process of transculturation to transpose the themes of class inequality from second-century BCE Rome to another extremely class-conscious society, Victorian London.[39] In these adaptations, Plautus' subtle critique of the powers that be is replaced by support for the status quo, while those who question authority and seek for a more equitable society are lampooned—not surprising for a school that has been referred to as "The King's Nurseries."[40] However, in their own ways, both Plautus' original and the

Westminster productions of *Trinummus* show us that maintaining a firm grip on moral superiority with one hand while shutting out the poor with the other has long been an aristocratic prerogative.

The Trouble with Influencers

In the reviews of the Westminster productions of *Trinummus*, the praise and blame all depend on taking the moralizing seriously, but what if that is not how it was intended to be understood at all? Scholarly reception of the play has been split between those who see the moral speeches and sententiae as sincere and those who see them as humorous. For example, Lessing (1749) and Ribbeck (1887) praised the morals of the play in similar fashion to the positive reviews of the Westminster performances, an approach that certainly fits the zeitgeist of the eighteenth and nineteenth centuries.[41] Segal sees the moralizing as boring but still earnest, a necessary expedient for a playwright who had to please the aediles in charge of selecting plays for the festival.[42] Some scholars have even argued that Plautus takes sides with notorious senate conservative Cato the Elder, an assertion that certainly strains belief and perhaps more than anything shows how diversely a single text can be interpreted over time.[43] On the other hand, Lefèvre argues that Plautus criticizes Cato and his brand of public moralizing, by pointing out the hypocrisy in the moral speeches in the play.[44] Moore also maintains that moral elements of *Trinummus* are satirical, and he even suggests that a key component of Plautine dramaturgy throughout the corpus is a programmatic rejection of comedy's ability to provide moral edification.[45] When scholarly opinions are divided to such an extent, the best approach is to go to the text and see what literary and philological analysis can tell us. When we dig into the details of *Trinummus*, it becomes evident that the moralizing passages can only be taken as sincere when they are clipped from their context and presented as soundbites. When taken in context, there are too many factors in the performance that undermine any sincerity that the characters might try to express. To illustrate this, we will examine Megaronides' monologues in the opening scene, the dialogue between Lysiteles and Philto, and Stasimus' moralizing speech near the end of the play.

Megaronides' speeches that bookend the opening scene provide a useful model for how to read the moralizing elements throughout. Megaronides begins by announcing that he has the responsibility to chastise his friend Callicles for his bad behavior, but he quickly proceeds to the general topos of bad morals that spring up like weeds everywhere you look:

> Here a disease has besieged good morals to such a degree
> that most all of them are now deceased.
> But while they fall ill, the bad morals in the meantime
> have sprung up abundantly, just like well-watered weeds—
> you can go cut down a colossal crop of them.
> Yes, nothing at all is cheap here except bad morals.
> Too often here, a part of the people considers the favor of the few
> worth more than that which benefits the bulk of us.
> In this way, favors conquer that which is conducive to the public good.
> In many matters, these despicable favors get in the way and
> cause a delay to both private wealth as well as the commonwealth.
>
> (28–38)

The speech sounds like something that could be spoken in the Senate or the Forum by those, like Cato, who were eager to return to strict Roman values in the face of increasing luxury and foreign influence. There is even a clever reference to the Republic in the phrase *rei privatae et publicae* in line 38, reminding the audience that the "here" (*hic*) that Megaronides repeatedly mentions is Rome for Plautus' audience.[46] Megaronides highlights the word *mores* (morals, customs, character), which was an important catchphrase in Roman politics and paints a dire image of a plague attacking traditional morals, a theme to which he returns in lines 72–6, when he finally begins to explain his complaint against Callicles.

It's a fine enough speech, if you like that sort of thing, but the problem is that the subsequent action proves that Megaronides has entirely misread the situation. He sees Callicles' purchase of the house from Lesbonicus as a symptom of this plague afflicting public morals, but in reality Callicles has stood by his absent friend Charmides, no matter what people were saying, and he maintained his trust or *fides*, which is another important catchphrase for the Romans.[47] This opening monologue by Megaronides introduces the theme of morals, but then the subsequent scene immediately proves the moral posturing to be ineffective and inaccurate.

In his second monologue that follows the scene with Callicles, Megaronides admits that, in taking his seemingly principled stance, he had actually fallen victim to the wiles of the *scurrae* (199–222). This is one of those difficult words to translate—dictionaries suggest things like fop, dandy, roustabout, or man-about-town, which aren't particularly helpful. For the Romans, this word represented the idle, city-dwelling busybodies who always have to be on top of the latest fashion and the latest gossip—the influencers, we might say:[48]

> The ones who pretend to know everything, but actually know nothing.
> They know what the king whispered in the queen's ear,
> They know what Juno said when she was with Jupiter,
> What each person thinks or is about to think, they know that too.
> If it never happened, never will happen, it doesn't matter. They still know it.
>
> (205–9)

There is a preachiness to this speech as well, though Megaronides does admit that he was in the wrong to pounce on an innocent friend for punishment (*prosilui amicum castigatum innoxium*). Lefèvre points out that the word *castigare*, used here and elsewhere by Megaronides, is frequently used to discuss the work of Roman censors, and he further contends that the hypocrisy shown by Megaronides could be a jab at Cato and those in his faction who made political careers of railing in public against things like wealth and influence, while they continued to amass these same things privately. Of course, Cato wouldn't be named censor until 184 BCE, the year of Plautus' death, but Lefèvre maintains that Cato's bid for the censorship was a defining feature of Roman politics in the decade between Cato's consulship in 195 and his appointment as censor.[49] Whether the critique in these bookended speeches is aimed specifically at Cato or just at the type of political discourse that Cato represented, Plautus nevertheless encourages his viewers at the outset of the play to be on the lookout for how the moral messages of the characters prove to be hypocritical and ultimately distract from the real issues at work in the plot.

Philto's Twenty-One Habits for Highly Pretentious People

Next up onstage are Lysiteles and his father Philto, who continue to build on the moralizing theme. Lysiteles starts the scene with a song-and-dance number about the evils of love (223–75). There is humorous incongruity here between the subject matter and the mode of presentation, like when Fred Astaire dances to the song "I won't Dance," especially if the audience is familiar with other second-act musical numbers from Plautus, like the very similar scene from *Mostellaria* (84–156) in which a comparable young man sings about how he has given in to love and debauchery.[50] When all we have is words on a page, it is easy to forget how important the music and movement would have been in the performances that the Romans watched. Lysiteles' song and dance about rejecting love could easily come across as a kind of comic praeteritio, with the actor claiming to reject the typical *adulescens* ethos, while still embracing all the musical fun of such characters in performance.[51]

When Philto comes out to join his son, we get the highest concentration of moral sententiae in the play—twenty-one in just the first scene with his son! Sententiae are one- or two-line quotable quotes on moral topics, the kind of thing one finds on motivational calendars or posters in the human resources office. Deciding what counts as a sententia is somewhat subjective. Sometimes they are acknowledged with phrases like "as the saying goes," but more often one must simply examine the text for generalizing statements that express a moral viewpoint; often they come at the beginning or end of a speech and explain a given character's choices.[52] According to my tally there are fifty-five sententiae in *Trinummus* comprising 87 lines, mostly centralized in the first two thirds of the play, though as I said, when you count them up your mileage may vary. When it comes to variety, there are bumper-sticker quotes in this collection for every taste and occasion:

For the philosophical:
He who seeks to be an artisan of the life well lived needs much practice at his art.

(365)

For the kind-hearted:
That which I have, I am eager that all my friends have it too.

(54)

For the vindictive:
It's awful when you're not allowed to avenge ill deserts as they deserve.

(1173)

For the prudish:
Love never attempts to cast its snares around anyone except a libidinous man.

(237)

For the downright celibate:
It is sheer madness to check in at the domicile of Desire.

(637)

For the social climber:
It is best to be the best, but if you can't, at least get married to one.

(486–7)

For the zealot:
He who constantly condemns himself is the one with a true talent for diligence.

(322)

For the wise youngster:
Age is just the seasoning for wisdom.
(368)

For the old wise guy:
Wisdom is the main course for age.
(368)

For the fiscally conservative:
If you give a beggar something to eat or drink you behave badly, since you lose what you gave and only extend the beggar's miserable life.
(339–40)

For the social activist:
Good will is wasted without good works.
(439)

For the delightfully gluttonous:
No point being bashful at the dinner table—that's where we separate the mortals from the gods.
(478–9)

or

A dinner invitation when grocery prices are this high is an inheritance tax-free.
(484)

This is a just a selection of the moral wit that *Trinummus* serves up; the full list is available in Appendix C. The Romans were big fans of these prepackaged moral tidbits and numerous collections of them circulated around the ancient world, some even under the names of comic playwrights, like Menander. While it wasn't seen as incongruous for such *sententiae* to appear in comedies, there is something off about the way they are employed in *Trinummus*.[53] Papaioannou points out that the quantity and concentration of the moral material in *Trinummus* hints at satire.[54] Nowhere is this better evinced than in the character of Philto, whose dialogue frequently reads like a patchwork of leftover moral maxims. Take, for example, this hefty helping of advice he gives to Lysiteles:

> If a man overcomes his passion, while he lives, we will be proclaimed conqueror of conquerors.
> If you overcome your passion rather than letting your passion overcome you, then you have a cause to rejoice.
> It is much better to be as you ought to be, rather than as your passion dictates.
> Those who conquer their passion are always proclaimed better than those whose passion conquers them.
>
> (309–12)

These lines read as if Plautus just tore a page right out of one of the collections of sententiae, from the chapter about passion [*animus*]. Any of these lines alone seems sufficient for the dialogue and if taken separately out of context, each could be quite sincere. It is, if course, possible that they are performance variants and that an actor would just choose one of the lines to say in an actual performance, but what if we take the repetition as intentional? In the concentration that we get these sententiae, especially from Philto, it seems that when the social conservatives asked for a comedy adorned with moral instruction, Plautus instead opened the moralizing firehose on them.

Besides the quantity of Philto's moral maxims, which suggests satire, certain details of the subsequent discussion with Lysiteles undercut the ideals Philto expresses early on. When Lysiteles tries to convince his father to allow him to marry without a dowry because it is the right thing to do for a friend who is destitute, Philto, rather than basing his decision on the morals he has espoused, instead makes up his mind according to the potential for reputation, favors, and social alliances (*fama*, *gratia*, and *amicitia*), the same things Megaronides labeled as threats to public and private prosperity in his opening speech.[55] When Philto agrees to arrange the marriage for his son, his moral pontification is further vitiated by the transformation of his character from the harsh old man, or *senex durus*, to the *senex lepidus*, the old man who works to help the love plot succeed, as discussed in Chapter 2. Although Philto's dialogue throughout the play is replete with phrases that, in the words of the nineteenth-century reviewer, "express the highest ethics of the pre-Christian Pagan world," in the end, as Moore states, "The audience is far more likely to be amused than moved by [Philto's] harangue."[56]

Stasimus has the Last Word

The focus on moralizing discourse continues through the scene about the marriage arrangements with Philto and Lesbonicus (402–601), including Stasimus' humorous versions of *sententiae* about the dinner table and grocery prices quoted above (478–9, 484). Morals are again a central component of the argument between Lysiteles and Lesbonicus over the dowry (622–718), though here with longer moral speeches and fewer *sententiae*. After that, there is a long break in the moralizing content, with virtually nothing in the plotting scene with the old men (729–819) and the failed deception with Charmides and the conman (820–1007). When we understand the *sententiae* and moralizing speeches as jokes based on repetition, then we can see in this evidence of Plautus' expert grasp of comic timing.

When you repeat a joke, the first three or four times are funny. At about five repetitions, it gets annoying for the audience, but if the actors push through this tedium to ten or more repetitions, then the laughter runs riot. We can see this principle working on a smaller scale with the repetition of the phrase "Just go" [*i modo*] in lines 580–90, where one or both of these words are repeated thirteen times in 11 lines. After the third or fourth "Just go" from Stasimus, the audience sighs, "Okay, we're going to keep doing this," but when we get to line 590, which ends with "Just go, just go, just go!" [*i modo, i modo, i modo!*], it is absolutely hilarious. There is then a break of a little over 10 lines, after which Callicles, who wasn't onstage for all the repetitions of *i modo*, begins his line with the almost identical *quo modo* [how], which wouldn't normally be funny, but given the comic setup, this word would get the biggest laugh of them all.[57] You can compare this to the very similar but longer scene in *Rudens* with the repetition of the word "okay" [*licet*, 1205–26], followed by Gripus' use of the same word at the beginning of the following scene (1227).

The repetition of moralizing speeches and *sententiae* in *Trinummus* functions on this same principle of intermittent repetition, but on a larger scale, stretching throughout the entire play. It is funny at first when Megaronides' moralizing is undercut by his misunderstanding of the situation. It may start to get tedious when every other line from Philto sounds like a moralizing soundbite. But when moralizing continues to be a key component in the debates about the marriage and dowry, the repetition could be extremely funny by this point. This would especially be true if the actors all used similar posture, gestures, or tone when delivering their moral wisdom. Plautus then lets the joke rest for some 300 lines, getting ready for his big moralizing finale.

Now, enter Stasimus, running across the stage at top speed, hurling abuse at himself for his tardy and disordered state. He can't believe he let himself get robbed by his drinking buddies at some seedy bar—remember, he left to collect money a friend owed him, an entire talent, so he says. With Charmides eavesdropping from the sidelines, Stasimus, drunk and disoriented, strikes that familiar pose at center stage and proclaims:

> If only the venerable old morals [*mores*] of mankind, that venerable austerity,
> could be held in more honor here than bad morals [*mores*] ...
> For customs [*mores*] now care not for what is permitted, only for what is pleasing:
> By custom [*more*], campaign fraud is sanctioned, it is free from laws;
> By custom [*more*], people are permitted to cast aside their shield, flee the enemy;
> By custom [*more*], people seek honor through disgrace ...
> By custom [*more*], the stronger, more active are passed over for office
> ...
> Customs [*mores*] have now brought the laws under their authority

and the laws are more beholden to them than ... than parents are to
   their children!
Those awful laws are now affixed to the wall with iron nails,
where it would be much better to hang up bad morals [*mores*].
                                                    (1028–9, 1032–40)

The speech continues in this fashion, for 11 more lines, until Stasimus meanders back to the theme of lending and reminds himself of the money he went to collect. Rhetorically, Plautus pulls out all the stops in this speech, with the anaphora of morals/customs [*more(s)*] paired with a catalog of Roman conservative buzzwords, like austerity [*parsimonia*, 1028], honor [*honos*, 1029, 1035], disgrace/crime [*flagitium*, 1035], and trustworthiness [*fides*, 1048]. When taken out of context, this speech seems to represent the noblest sentiments of the play. With its repetition of themes and language from the earlier speeches by Megaronides, Philto, and Lysiteles, it comes across as an excellent finale to the moral theme.

But what happens when we consider the context of this speech? First of all, the speech is constantly interrupted by asides from Charmides, who is eavesdropping on the whole affair. For the most part, Charmides just expresses his agreement with Stasimus' diatribe, with phrases like "A disgusting custom!" [*morem inprobum*, 1035—another use of *mores*] and "Certainly horrible!" [*nequam quidem*, 1036]. Even these agreements could have a comic effect if the actor playing Charmides also played Megaronides and Philto, as I suggest in Chapter 2—then we would have the arch-moralizer of the play corroborating Stasimus' sudden turn to ethics. Charmides also gets the final two moral maxims in the play, 1173 and 1185, which would also be a fitting curtain call for the Megaronides/Philto actor. Charmides' approval of Stasimus, however, has to be seen as tongue in cheek, since some of his remarks serve to highlight the incongruity between the content of the speech and the speaker. In 1030, Charmides exclaims that Stasimus is speaking of "kingly affairs," using the Greek loan word *basilica*, which is frequently used in Plautus to mark the behavior of enslaved individuals as pretentious or in some way transgressing their place in society.[58] He then asserts that Stasimus' love of the venerable old ways [*vetera*] must come from his love of *mos maiorum* [custom of the ancestors], likely the most prominent phrase for encapsulating traditional Roman virtues. The only problem here is that Stasimus, as a slave, legally did not have ancestors (*nullo patre* was the legal phrase), so the assertion that he embraces *mos mairoum* is a joke about his social status, one that Plautus repeats in other plays.[59] Overall, the comments by Charmides emphasize the inconsistency between Stasimus as speaker and the ideals that he expresses.

In addition to Charmides' asides, Stasimus' introduction to the monologue should preclude us from taking any of his moral sentiments seriously (1008–27). He enters in typical running-slave fashion, yet he lacks any real need for the haste.[60] He blames himself repeatedly for his behavior, calling himself a worthless human being [*homo nihili*, 1013, 1017], after which he admits that he got tanked in a tawdry dive bar [*in thermopolio*] and lost his ring [*condalium es oblitus*, 1013–14]. The highlight though is Stasimus' wild catalog of drinking buddies: *Struthus fuit, Circonychus, Cremnus, Cercobulus, Collabus*.[61] The easiest choice for dealing with these names is to leave them untranslated, as de Melo does in the Loeb, but we miss a big component of the humor if we don't have an idea of the mash-up of Greek words that Plautus uses here. *Struthus* comes from the Greek word for "sparrow" [στρουθός] and it can be used as slang for the penis and refer to someone who displays lewd behavior generally (think Catullus' infamous *passer* here).[62] My translation: Lil' Pecker. Circonychus is a compound word consisting of the Greek word for "hawk" (κίρκος), and another word that could be "claw" (ὄνυξ) or "night" (νύξ). Alternatively, this name could be spelled with -*nicus* at the end, derived from the Greek word for "victory" (νική), and mean someone who beats hawks, as de Melo and Gratwick suggest. While Hawkbeater is an interesting enough sobriquet, the first half of the name could also be derived from the Greek word for "tail" (κέρκος), which is also slang for penis. In English, if we use the word "cock," we can combine the bird imagery with the phallic imagery. My translation: Nightcock.[63] Cremnus comes from the Greek word for "cliff" or "crag" (κρημνός), thus associating the name with an idea of danger, but

Hippocrates (*Loc. Hom.* 47) uses this same word to describe female genitalia, specifically the labia. My translation: Ladylips.⁶⁴ In Cercobulus we again see the Greek word for "tail/penis" (κέρκος) combined with a suffix that derives from the Greek word βούλομαι, which means "to think, contemplate, or consider." My translation: Dick-for-brains. Finally, Collabus comes from Greek κόλλοψ, a noun meaning "peg" or "screw," but in some comic fragments the word seems to refer to transvestite or intersex prostitutes.⁶⁵ My translation: Peggy. When we add these names to our translation, this is what we get:

> Did you really lose your memory after three drinks? Or was it
>   because you were there dinking with such upstanding fellows,
> the kind of guys who could easily keep their hands off other people's
>   stuff?
> Let's see, there was Lil' Pecker, Nightcock, Ladylips, Dick-for-brains,
>   and Peggy!
> Purse-snatching, shackle-cracking, chain-chafing whipping posts!
> Do you really intend to ask for your little ring back from those guys?
> One of them snatched the shoe from a runner in mid-stride, while I
>   was right there!

While the language surrounding the catalog of names emphasizes expertise at thievery, the names themselves hint at questionable sexual behavior for the Romans, as does the reference to the ring. Gratwick has noted that Plautus connects this scene with the title character of his play *Curculio*, who also makes a running entrance and delivers a bombastic speech about public morals (*Curculio* 280–370).⁶⁶ In that scene, Curculio brags about stealing a signet ring from a soldier during a dice game at a bar. Later in the play, the pimp Cappadox makes fun of the soldier for losing his little ring [*anulum*], which indicates he must be part of a disbanded [*expunctum*] military unit (583–5). Plautus, always the clever wordsmith, uses double entendre with these words: *anulum* is the diminutive for anus and the verb *pungo* can be used as slang for sexual penetration, thus Cappadox' word choice suggests that the soldier has "hurt his little asshole in the buggered brigade."⁶⁷

In the scene from *Trinummus*, Plautus uses a different word when Stasimus talks about his ring, *condalium* instead of *anulum*, but the similarities between the scenes can connect Stasimus' lost ring with Cappadox' insults. Taking all these details together, the shout-out to Curculio, the mention of the lost ring, and the sexual valence behind the names of Stasimus' drinking buddies give an air of sexual deviance to whatever happened in the *thermopolium*. Furthermore, since Plautus invites us to compare Stasimus with Curculio, Stasimus' loss of the ring is an inversion of Curculio's theft of the ring, and one more way in which Plautus emphasizes Stasimus' inability to live up to the deceptive potential of his character type, as explored in Chapter 2.

With an introduction like this, it is virtually impossible to take Stasimus' moralizing in the scene seriously. Plautus has taken the sentiments of Cato or one of his colleagues and focalized them through a truant, tipsy slave who has narrowly escaped some sort of sinister roadhouse encounter, "a most incongruent proponent of such morality," as Moore concludes.[68] What better way to emphasize the hypocrisy of the moralizing faction in Roman politics and society. Plautus saves his most outrageous and daring deconstruction of Roman moralizing for the last.

Conclusion

If one looks to *Trinummus* for authentic moral instruction and is willing to clip lines from their context, it is perhaps possible to claim: "Either Plautus or his Greek prototype Philemon must have drunk very deeply at the philosophic fountains Greek thought."[69] I, however, prefer to think that Plautus slipped on a banana peel and did a pratfall into "the philosophic fountains of Greek thought," and what we get in *Trinummus* is his playful splashing about.

Conclusion

In *Mostellaria*, another play that Plautus adapted from a Greek original by Philemon, the young lover Philolaches sings a rousing song about how people are like houses: dutiful parents build them sturdy and strong, sound behavior keeps them in good repair, but bad habits ruin them and the storms of love can seep in and rot the timbers, which is what has happened to this particular young man (84–156). As the play progresses, the house becomes a metaphor for the character of Philolaches and for the plot as a whole. In *Trinummus*, we also get a house at center stage that serves as a metaphor for the plot and characters. It appears to have fallen on hard times. We actually see, as the play begins, the embodiment of hopeless destitution as she moves into the dwelling, supposedly to stay. But all is not as it seems. Inside this house there is a treasure, a treasure that draws friends together to support an absent neighbor, ensures the protection of the younger generation and the continuation of the household, and even provides an impetus for the comic deception plot, so important in Roman comedy. Despite the outward appearance, wealth is hidden within, more than enough to solve everyone's problems—but some excavation is required!

The house of Charmides can stand as a metaphor for the play itself and its reception history in scholarship and performance. It was a shabby house, sold for a discount cash price, largely left derelict by performers and scholars, unless they wanted to stop by and throw a few rocks through the windows. But for those willing to do a little digging, there are treasures to be found in *Trinummus*. For some, these are treasures of moral wisdom, the kind that helped keep a tradition of Latin performance at a school alive during uncertain times. For others, that same moralizing material can offer humor and a glimpse of a master satirist commenting on the political discourse of his day. When we consider the play within the context of Roman comedy generally, we can see that *Trinummus* pushes the boundaries of plot and characterization, while at the same time commenting on the genre on a larger scale than typical Plautine metatheater. *Trinummus* deconstructs and rearranges the typical comic plot and stock characters, and tests us to see if we recognize the games it plays.

For those in search of what is Roman in Roman comedy, *Trinummus* certainly offers a treasure trove. References to rituals and prayers situate the play within a nexus of performances at Rome that are religious, theatrical, and social. The incongruent character of Lesbonicus and the absence of Charmides can help place us in the middle of the ancient audience in the Forum, where we can watch Plautus offer average Romans an image of the kind of outcome that they desperately desired while husbands, fathers, and brothers were away on campaign. For the adventurous director or performer, a wealth of humor can be found in the play, if they are willing to search for modern equivalents to Plautus' experimental stock character amalgamations and playful destabilization of moral discourse. *Trinummus* is funny and compelling—it deserves to be back on the stage!

We started our discussion of *Trinummus* by framing it as an underdog story. Hopefully in reading this analysis of the play, you have found ways to see *Trinummus* in a new light and appreciate the experimental, metatheatrical treasure hunt that Plautus sends us on. Don't be fooled by the paltry three coins of the title. There is more here than expected. After all, Plautus wanted it that way (8–9, 18–21).

Appendix A: Music in *Trinummus*

Roman comedy was a very musical genre, though this can be difficult to tell from translations. Plautus used various meters throughout each of his plays and we can detect and label these meters by scanning the long and short syllables in each line. We know from annotations in manuscripts and evidence from various ancient authors that certain meters were accompanied by music and others were not. During the accompanied sections, a musician onstage would play an instrument called a tibia, a kind of double clarinet, and the actors would sing their lines in some fashion. Analysis of the meter can tell us the rhythm of these songs, but there is no way of recreating the melodies since no decipherable musical annotation for these plays besides the meter has survived. When analyzing the meter and music in Roman comedy, we can label each scene using a system of three registers: 1) spoken, for passages with no musical accompaniment; 2) recitative, for passages with accompaniment and a meter of standard length; and 3) songs in mixed meters, for passages in which the meter changes constantly. The pace of Roman comedy in performance was dictated by regular alternations between accompanied and unaccompanied scenes.

The only meter used for the spoken passages is the iambic senarius, a line that contains six iambs. An iamb is a short syllable followed by a long syllable, though in practice many substitutions were allowed. There was a variety of meters used for the accompanied recitative passages, but the one most important for *Trinummus* is the trochaic septenarius, a line that contained seven and a half trochees (long–short), also with many substitutions permitted. *Trinummus* also contains a few sections with anapests (short–short–long), an accompanied meter that can be used to complement swift movement onstage or mark important entrances and exits. While we know the recitative meters were accompanied by the tibia, we are not entirely sure how the actors delivered the lines, whether they sang them with distinct melodies, repeated a set melody over and over again, or chanted them in some way along to the music. The songs in mixed meters featured a wide variety of constantly changing lyric meters set to fanciful and inventive language. They would have been big song-and-dance numbers that allowed star performers to shine with impressive solos and duets.

For the metrical analysis of *Trinummus* below, I have used bold font for the accompanied passages to demonstrate visually the interplay between the scenes that are spoken and scenes that are sung.

Line numbers	Meter	Description
1–222	Iambic senarii	The prologue and expository scene with Megaronides and Callicles is spoken
223–300	**Mixed meters**	**The big song-and-dance number for the play is Lysiteles' song about rejecting love. At line 276, he is joined by Philto, and the song continues as a duet until line 300.**
301–91	**Trochaic septenarii**	**The musical accompaniment continues, but the register changes to recitative when Lysiteles tells his father his plans to marry without a dowry.**
392–601	Iambic senarii	The music stops when we meet Lesbonicus and Stasimus and the spoken register continues through their scene with Philto. This helps mark Lesbonicus as a blocking character and emphasizes the ineffectiveness of Stasimus' mini deception about the farm.
602–728	**Trochaic septenarii**	**The music returns when Callicles finds out about the marriage proposal and continues through the scene between Lysiteles and Lesbonicus, marking movement toward the love plot and giving Lysiteles another chance to sing.**
729–819	Iambic senarii	When Megaronides and Callicles plan the deception, the meter changes back to a spoken register, which is uncommon for scenes of plotting and foreshadows the failure of their scheme.

820–42	Anapests	Charmides' surprise return is marked by recitative anapests.
843–997	Trochaic septenarii	There is musical accompaniment when Charmides defeats the conman, thus marking the old man as one of the prime tricksters in the play.
998–1007	Iambic senarii	The music stops briefly while Charmides expresses his concerns after the conman has left.
1008–92	Trochaic septenarii	**Stasimus turns the music back on with his unexpected running-slave entrance and parodic moralizing speech.**
1093–114	Iambic senarii	The scene switches back to the spoken register for the important revelation that Callicles has kept the house and the treasure safe for Charmides.
1115–19	Anapests	**Lysiteles' triumphant entry after hearing of the return of Charmides is marked by a brief five lines of anapest.**
1120–89	Trochaic septenarii	**The success of the love plot and the denouement is accompanied in recitative septenarii.**

For further reading on meter and music in Roman comedy, see Duckworth 1994: 361–83; Marshall 2006: 203–44; Moore 2012a; Moore 2012b; Moore 1998b.

Appendix B: A Textual Note on Line 831

Line 831 reads "may [the gods] always be kind to the poor" [*semper mendicis modesti sint*]. Most editors put square brackets around this line, meaning that they believe it should be deleted from the text.[1] Usually, editors do this when there are issues in the manuscripts, like when a particularly reliable manuscript doesn't include a certain line. Lines can also be bracketed when there are syntactical problems that can't be worked out through simple emendations, thus suggesting that the manuscript reading is corrupt and unintelligible. For the line in question here, there are no syntactical reasons to delete it—it expresses a wish in the subjunctive and it follows syntactically and thematically from the end of the previous line, with the plural subject of *sint* being implied from the plural *dis* in the phrase *hoc dis dignum est* [this is worthy of the gods].[2] Nor are there any issues with the manuscripts. In fact, due to an impressive digitization project by the Vatican Library, one can go online and easily view this passage in the best manuscript of Plautus, and the line is clearly legible there.[3]

So why do editors delete it? Mueller initially objected to the line because of a slight metrical abnormality, a long syllable that must be read as short in order to fit the anapestic meter, but this anomaly appears elsewhere in Plautus and should not be considered sufficient reason to delete a line that is well attested in the manuscripts.[4] The real reason seems to be more of an ideological one, as can be seen in the question that Leo asks about the line when he deletes it: "Why would [Charmides] include himself among the poor for no reason?" [*mendicis cur se adnumeret nulla causa?*].[5] As we saw in Chapter 3, the question of the property and social class to which Charmides and Lesbonicus belong is indeed central to an understanding of what the play could have meant to a Roman audience. The editors who favor deleting the line see Charmides as a typical wealthy old man from comedy, but let's not forget that we have been repeatedly told that he has been driven into poverty by his circumstances. Does it make more sense to see this prayer as the words of a wealthy man who doesn't need Neptune's help or as the thanksgiving of a poor man whose narrow success on this voyage has been guarded by a god who knows who needs his help most? The latter option fits best with the image of Charmides' family that we see elsewhere in the play, one that is trying to make it in the world of the *nobiles* but does not belong to the same social class [*ordo*] and property class [*factio*] as Philto and Lysiteles. While it is true that in line 839, at the end of the prayer, Charmides tells us that he completed this voyage to obtain riches for his son, he doesn't comment on how successful this was, besides his determination to dedicate himself to leisure [*otium*] from here on out (838). Instead, when he believes that Callicles has cheated Lesbonicus out of the house, he feels that the family fortunes are utterly ruined (1087–91). "Now here I die destitute" [*nunc hic disperii miser*, 1089], he declares, before Callicles enters and explains how the situation really stands. In response to Leo's question, we see that there are actually very good reasons for Charmides to count himself among the poor who hope to benefit from Neptune's aid.

Gray, expanding on Leos' reasoning, claims that, since Charmides is wealthy, line 831 has no place in the text. He further argues that line 830 indicates a rejection of the idea that the gods spare the poor and tame the wealthy: "you [Neptune] do not *divites damnas atque domas* [curse and curb the wealthy] but treat each with the respect that is his due."[6] Here we see one of the occasional shortcomings of nineteenth-century textual criticism—aristocratic scholars projecting their values onto the text. In their minds, of course Neptune would support the status quo and keep people from "rising above their station." What is remarkable in this instance is that this conviction was strong enough to lead them to delete a perfectly legible line from an ancient text. To be fair, we all inevitably write and interpret from our own perspective, despite the lenses we attempt to use to help us see the ancient world from the point of view of those who lived in it. I readily admit that my background as a first-generation college student from blue-color suburbia inflects the messages I see in texts, including this passage from *Trinummus*. Nevertheless, when the philological evidence is weighed, with bias set aside, there is not sufficient reason to remove the line from the text.

Appendix C: Moral Sententiae in *Trinummus*

Below are all the passages that I identified as moral sententiae in *Trinummus*, listed by line number. Only one is explicitly marked in the text (351–2, *scin quid cantari solet*, "you know what they are accustomed to say, don't you?"). I chose the rest based on the moralizing content and the gnomic qualities of the text—i.e., generic second- or third-person subjects, no reference to specific characters, jingling tone in Latin, etc. Different readers may come up with different lists in this process.

Moral Sententiae

23–5 It is an unpleasant task to punish a friend deservedly for a fault, but sometimes it is useful and profitable.

32 Nothing is cheap here except for bad morals.

34–5 Here part of the people considers the favor of the few worth more than that which benefits the many.

54 That which I have, I am eager that all my friends have it too.

63 A known evil is the best one.

78 All good men and women ought to take care to keep themselves away from suspicion and blame.

81–2 I am the guardian of my own heart, so that I don't deserve any blame, but suspicion lies in the heart of another.

95–6 If you know that I have done something unwise or incorrect, if you don't accuse me, you yourself are to blame.

145 Whatever you leave in my care, you can pick it up again where you left it.

169–71 The wolf watches until the dogs are sleeping. He is hungrier and his mouth gapes more fiercely, he wants to devour the entire flock.

237–237b Love never attempts to cast its snares around anyone except a libidinous man.

255 While he is being obliging, the lover himself becomes destitute.

257 When a person is poor, he is worth so little.

260 Love can give bitter things too.

265a–266 He who falls headlong into love, perishes worse than if he jumped from a cliff.

271–2 Good people seek these things for themselves: wealth, trust, honor, glory, and good favor; this is the reward for the honorable.

273–4 I would rather live among the honorable than with the idle-chattering scoundrels.

284 The bad want the good to be bad, so that they are more like themselves.

286–286a A covetous generation considers the sacred profane and the private public.

288–9 The things which they are unable to touch with their hand, those alone do they consider it right to keep their hands off of. For the rest, they steal, drag off, runaway, and hide.

293–4 These men praise their ancestors, but they defile the very ones whom they praise.

299 I don't care for those morals that are more like dregs, the murky ones with which the "good people" disgrace themselves.

309 If a man overcomes his passion, while he lives, he will be proclaimed conqueror of conquerors.

Appendix C: Moral Sententiae in Trinummus

310 If you overcome your passion rather than letting your passion overcome you, then you have a cause to rejoice.

311 It is much better to be as you ought to be, rather than as your passion dictates.

312 Those who conquer their passion are always proclaimed better than those whose passion conquers them.

320 He alone is honorable, who is dissatisfied with how honorable he is.

321 He who is satisfied with himself is neither honorable nor upright.

322 He who constantly condemns himself is the one with a true talent for diligence.

323 Cover you good deeds with more good deeds, so the rain doesn't seep through.

339-40 If you give a beggar something to eat or drink you behave badly, since you lose what you gave and only extend the beggar's miserable life.

343 Have pity on others only to the extent that others won't have to pity you.

345 Letter for letter, it's better to feel shame than to feel sorry.

347-8 When you do good to a friend, you're not sorry you did it, but you feel shame if you don't do it.

351-2 That which you have, may you not have, and that which you don't have may you have, namely punishment, since you are unable to enjoy yourself nor allow anyone else to enjoy themselves either.

354 He who has nothing with which to do his duty is not doing his duty.

361 Many things happen to a man which he wants and which he doesn't want.

363–4 It is the wise man who fashions fortune for himself; many things which he doesn't want don't happen for him, unless he is a bad craftsman.

365 He who seeks to be an artisan of the life well lived needs much practice at his art.

367 Not by age but by character is wisdom obtained.

368 Age is the seasoning of wisdom, but wisdom is the main course for age.

395–9 The one who provides as counsel against his son nothing other than what is pleasing to himself, is wasting his time. He becomes wretched in his soul and accomplishes more than nothing. He prepares a more bitter winter for himself since he stirs up that savage storm.

439 Good will is wasted without good works.

461–2 Foolish words and foolish deeds, neither are much use at any age.

478–9 No point being bashful at the dinner table—that's where we separate the mortals from the gods.

484 A dinner invitation when grocery prices are this high is an inheritance tax-free.

486–7 It's best to be the best, but if you can't, at least get married to one.

490–4 The gods are wealthy; wealth and factions are fitting for them. But we mere mortals, as soon as we lose what little life we have, the poor man and the wealthiest are assigned to the same tax bracket when they are dead.

620–21 It is extremely difficult to find a friend worthy of the name, to whom you could entrust your affairs and sleep without a care.

673 It is sheer madness to check in at the domicile of Desire.

684 Never will a person be taken seriously among strangers who renders himself insignificant among his own family

697 It is an honor for the virtuous man to remember his duty.

Appendix C: Moral Sententiae in Trinummus

847 See what trouble poverty causes for a destitute man.

1130-1 A favor, when it is given to a person to be their own, is immediately gone, but that which is lent, you can get back whenever you want.

1173 It's awful when you're not allowed to avenge ill deserts as they deserve.

1185 A single misfortune is enough for one person.

Lines Likely Based on Moral Sententiae (but not Quoted Directly)

104-5 Don't live up to the slander.

129-32 Giving a lover money is like giving him a sword.

199-211 Ills of gossip.

279-80 Piety to fathers.

317 Obedience.

416-17 Thrift.

650-1 Pay attention to friends not girlfriends.

668-72 Love destroys character.

Moral Speeches

23-38 Megaronides.

199-222 Megaronides.

223-75 Lysiteles.

276-323 Lysiteles and Philto.

627-716 Lysiteles and Lesbonicus.

1028-59 Stasimus.

Notes

1 Introduction

1 While Titus Maccius Plautus sounds like a standard Roman name, it is certainly a comic pseudonym that translates to something like Dick Clownson Flatfoot. See Hanses 2020: 10–11 and n. 19.
2 By using the term "empire" here, I am not referring to the period that historians label as the Roman Empire (31 BCE to 476 CE), but rather to the project of empire, as understood in postcolonial theory. For a primer, see Tyson 2014: 398–447.
3 For descriptions of the festivals at which Roman comedy was presented and the overall context of these performances, see Dionysius of Halicarnassus 7.72 = Fabius Pictor Fragment 16; Manuwald 2011: 41–55; Marshall 2006: 16–48; Bernstein 2007; Goldberg 1998; Goldberg 2018.
4 An inability to serve in the military prevented a Roman from pursuing a political career as well, thus ensuring that actors could not engage in civic leadership. For more details and sources on Roman actors, see Manuwald 2011: 85–6, esp. n. 147. Regarding *infamia*, the basis of Roman citizenship was that it protected the Roman male body from undue abuse, like corporal punishment. Actors chose to put their bodies on display before the public, and not in the venerable way that orators and politicians did (the distinction here may be lost on modern observers). As a result of willingly forfeiting their protection as citizens, they also forfeited their voting rights. See Brown 2002.
5 Friedrich Leo, in 1912, discredited the story by comparing it to other ancient biographies, but Richlin argues that the details may give us insight into the difficulties of survival in Rome's theatrical undercast. Richlin 2017: 4–7.
6 Gratwick 1982: 95.
7 For a full discussion of the potential relationship between the texts of Plautus and improv performance, see Marshall 2006: 245–79.
8 For examples of Plautus providing material for social history, see Gruen 1996: 124–57; Gruen 2014.

9 Quoted in Lefèvre 1993: 178.
10 Segal 1974; Sharrock 2014.
11 Hutcheon and O'Flynn 2013.
12 Marshall 2006: 17.
13 De Melo 2013: 115; Slater 1987: 265; Livy 34.54.3.
14 Scott 2008.

2 Playing against Type: *Trinummus* as Roman Comedy Remix

1 Alison Sharrock calls these repetitive jokes pop-ups, see Sharrock 2009: 190–201.
2 Sharrock 2014: 172.
3 O'Bryhim 2020: 123–4.
4 *Lena* is a particularly difficult word to translate, and I wish there were better options than bawd or procuress. It is the female equivalent of *leno*, usually translated as pimp, and it refers to a woman who owns/manages a group of sex workers. For the difficulties of translation in discussions of Roman sex workers, see Witzke 2015.
5 NB in each category, the characters from *Trinummus* are listed as sometimes corresponding to each character type in question because they do not fully fit these character types, though on the surface it appears that they should.
6 Marshall 2006: 126–58.
7 There were two types of masks for female characters: old women with white hair and young women with dark hair.
8 Marshall 2006: 135. Periplectomenus from *Miles Gloriosus* is the *senex lepidus* par excellence in Plautus, but a distinction in mask would be undesirable for him since he twice has to play the *senex durus* in Palaestrio's plays-within-a-play (481–595; 1394–427). Since he enters the stage in character each time, he could possibly switch to an asymmetrical mask for each play-within-a-play, then don a mask with neutral eyebrows for his other scenes.
9 From hints in the text, it is possible that Pseudolus, Leonida (*Asinaria*), and Truculentus all wore the same red-haired mask with asymmetrical eyebrows that set them apart as a *servus callidus*. Marshall 2006: 133–4.

10 Duckworth 1994 (1st ed. 1952): 249–53; Segal 1968: 151; Sharrock 2009: 17.
11 Segal (1968) discusses the saturnalian aspects of Roman festivals and the plays presented therein, how there is usually an inverted social dynamic in the plays and a vivid distinction between the real world and the world of the plays, the forum vs the festival (ch. 2). Segal also elaborates the roles and identities of blocking characters in Plautus (ch. 3).
12 The unnamed daughter and the treasure are essentially synonymous in the play—unseen elements that enrich the household and move the plot forward (cf. *Aulularia*). Special thanks to Sharon James for sharing this perspective with me from some of her work in progress on daughters in Roman comedy.
13 In all quotations, the Latin text is from de Melo 2013 for *Trinummus* and Lindsay's Oxford edition for the rest of Plautus. The translations are my own, except when noted otherwise.
14 Timothy Moore explains how monologues, eavesdropping, and asides help characters build rapport with the audience. See Moore 1998a: 24–9, esp. 33–4.
15 See also *Miles* 1137–9, where the use of *circumspice* is connected with Palaestrio's humorous title *architectus*.
16 Moore 1998b: esp. 246.
17 Λυσιτελής, from the verb λυσιτελέω, which means "to bring profit or gain." Gray (1897: 86) argues that this name signals Lysiteles as a virtuous young man, which may be true, to the extent that focusing one's life on profit is a virtuous pursuit.
18 These words constituted a legally binding speech act. Plautus uses the full formula at *Amphitruo* 925–8. For further analysis, see Rosenmeyer 1995; Zagagi 1980.
19 Anderson 1979.
20 O'Bryhim 2020.
21 According to Erich Segal (1968: 42–70), the inverted social dynamic between slave and master in Plautus is part of an overall carnivalesque feel to the plays that fits in with the festival atmosphere at Rome, when typical rules and hierarchies are temporarily put on hold for the duration of the festival.
22 See Chapter 4 for an analysis of the religious parody in this scene.
23 In fact, *lepidus* is used alongside *comminiscor* in the example from *Miles* cited above (241).

24 For a thorough discussion of the metatheatrical aspects of Pseudolus's claims at playwrighting, see Slater 1985: 97–120.
25 The adjective *graphicus* is used twice in *Pseudolus* (519, 700), both times referring to Pseudolus as a quintessential trickster character. In *Persa*, *graphicus* is used three times, in close context with other words that mark comic scheming: 306—*graphice facetus*; 463-4—*lepida. . .graphice*; 843—*graphice hunc volo ludificari*. In *Trinummus*, besides this use by Megaronides, Charmides uses the adjective three times to describe the conman: 936, 1024, and 1139.
26 For *Trinummus* as experimental theater, see Papaioannou 2016.
27 The old man Demaenetus uses very similar language at *Asinaria* 71.
28 For further analysis of this scene, see Muecke 1985; Muecke 1986.
29 Moore 1998a: 26–49, esp. 33–4.
30 Charmides' asides include lines 876-7, 892, 895-6 (commented on but not overheard), 900, 904, 911, 929-30, 936-8 (commented on but not overheard), 958-63.
31 This is an example of an elastic gag. See Marshall 2006: 272-3.
32 For more discussion on the resonances between these scenes, see Petrone 2016: 29–33.
33 While the scheme with the conman does fail, the old men do meet their objective of protecting the property of their friend. See Papaioannou 2016: 181.
34 For a thorough discussion of the meters and music in Roman comedy, see Moore 2012; Moore 2012b; Moore 1998b.
35 One exception to this could have been *Menaechmi*, in which the set of twins would have been played by the same actor throughout, but then in the final recognition scene, a different actor would have donned the costume and mask of the second twin. See Damen 1989.
36 For role sharing in Plautus generally with some specific discussion of *Trinummus*, see Marshall 2006: 94–120, esp. 110 n. 84 and 119.
37 Papaioannou 2016: 176.

3 What's Roman about *Trinummus*?

1 Handley 1968.
2 Anderson 1993: 3–29; M. L. Damen 1992; Goldberg 1990; Marshall 2006: 3–4; Owens 1994.

3 Adler 2016: 45–6.
4 Adler 2016: 53–4; Pfeiffer 1976: 174–6.
5 Pfeiffer 1976: 173–5.
6 The emphasis on sources fits in well with the zeitgeist of the time, as also seen in the fields of historical linguistics and comparative mythology. Linguists, beginning with Sir William Jones, began reconstructing the linguistic ancestor of Greek, Latin, and Sanskrit, ultimately recreating a lost language that we now call Proto-Indo-European. Interestingly, this project also relied on the search for lost/unknown/unknowable originals. This search for linguistic connections within the Indo-European language family also led to heightened interest in comparative anthropological and mythological studies, especially ones that proved connections between cultures that were related as members of the Indo-European language family. See Csapo 2005: 10–79.
7 Pfeiffer 1976: 170.
8 Ferrary 2006.
9 The Cairo Codex was published in 1907, the Bodmer Codex including the entire play of *Dyskolos* was published in 1959, with more fragments published in 1965 and 1969. See Handley 1968: 4; Miller 1987: 15.
10 Duckworth 1994: 384–5.
11 Leo 1895: 77. "Die landläufige Beurtheilung des Plautus thut ihm zu viel und zu wenig. Seine komödien sind nicht sein, und sie waren schöner und besser ehe er sie sich zu eigen machte; aber sein Stil ist gewachsen, wenn auch aus fremdem Lande verplantzt, doch im eigenen Erdreich." The translation is mine.
12 Qtd in Marshall 2008.
13 Beare 1933.
14 Norwood 1923: 1–2.
15 Anderson 1979: 339–44.
16 Hutcheon and O'Flynn 2013: 8–9.
17 Hutcheon and O'Flynn 2013: 145–52.
18 Of the twenty-one extant plays, nine indicate some information about the Greek originals in the prologue or production notes in the manuscripts: *Asinaria*—*Onagos* by Demophilus (10–12); *Casina*—*Kleroumenoi* by Diphilus (31–4); *Mercator*—*Emporos* by Philemon (9–10); *Miles*—*Alazon*, no author indicated (86); *Poenulus*—*Karchedonios*, no author indicated (53); *Rudens*—original written by Diphilus, no title indicated (32–3);

Stichus—*Adelphoe* by Menander (production notes); *Trinummus*—*Thesauros* by Philemon (18–19); *Vidularia*—*Schedia*, no author indicated (fr. 6–7). Much more information about the originals has been gleaned from other sources, but Plautus himself gives us information for almost half.

19 Hutcheon and O'Flynn 2013: 8.
20 Beard, North, and Price 1998: 19–22; Manuwald 2011: 15.
21 Manuwald 2011: 16–17.
22 Batstone 2006: 545.
23 Manuwald 2011: 18; Batstone 2006: 546.
24 Caecilius Statius was a comic poet who flourished between the careers of Plautus and Terence. For more analysis of this passage from Cicero, see Leigh 2004: 6–9.
25 Gabba 1989: 201–3.
26 Gabba 1989: 205–6.
27 Shelton 1998: 150.
28 Cato frag. 167, Gabba 1989: 203.
29 Gray argues that the prologue speakers always wore distinctive costumes that set them apart for this purpose (Gray 1897: xxxvii).
30 *Munus* can mean "duty," "service," or "office" and frequently refers to public office, especially when paired with *rei publicae* (e.g., Cicero *Pro Cluentio* 89.9, *de Provinciis Consularibus* 35.13, *de Divinatione* 2.4.11). *Fungor* is used to describe the action of fulfilling one's public office, as in the phrases *consulatu fungor* (Suetonius *Vita Divi Juli* 23.1.1; Tacitus *Annales* 1.39.7) and *aedilitate fungor* (Cicero *de Officiis* 2.57.10; Suetonius *de Grammaticis et Rhetoribus* 30.1; Tacitus *Annales* 6.30.5).
31 It is not infrequent for Plautus to announce the location of the action in the opening lines of the prologue—e.g., *Truculentus* 3, *Rudens* 33, *Miles* 88—but here he does not do this.
32 The closest we get to a description of Charmides as a merchant is his reference to paying the customs fee to the customs agent (*solutum est portitori iam portorium*, 1107), but even this is very vague.
33 Pay particular attention to the use of the word *res* to mean "wealth," "money," or "property" (Lewis and Short s.v. *res* II.B–C), as in the phrase *res publica*, "commonwealth." While *res* can mean many different things, in *Trinummus* it is used repeatedly to refer to wealth. See lines 13, 328, 336, 344(?), 446, 451, 507, 617, 621, 635(?), 636(?), 656, 682, 733, 1092 (question

marks indicate lines where *res* could be taken to mean "wealth" or could have a broader sense).

34 Furthermore, in the scene in which Charmides confronts the con artist sent by Megaronides, the latter's reference to his ridiculously long name (885–6) and catalog of adventures (928–47) is reminiscent of scenes with soldiers and their messengers. Cf. *Curculio* 406–52, *Miles* 1–78.

35 Cf. also line 255, in which Lysiteles says it is through generosity that lovers become destitute (*fit ipse, dum ille comis est, inops amator*).

36 Anderson 1979: 335–6. Anderson also notes that the lack of a love interest for Lesbonicus was first pointed out by Leo.

37 Plautus also uses this phrase in *Rudens* when Trachalio sarcastically applies it to Labrax the pimp (735). It is telling that the phrase is used in a debate about social status in which Trachalio argues that Palaestra and Ampelisca should be set free, since Palaestra is born from freeborn parents (*haec est nata Athenis ingenuis parentibus*, 738). A similar phrase, *adprime nobilis*, is used to describe the families of the young men in *Cistellaria* (125) and Ter. *Eunuchus* (952).

38 Brunt 1982.

39 Both *ordo* and *factio* could be used to refer to one's social class or standing; however, the addition of the genitive plural *rerum*, here translated as "wealth," clarifies that Lesbonicus is using these phrases to talk about two distinct categories for assessing one's position in society. *Factio*, at the time of Plautus, refers to social standing. Later on in Latin literature, it takes on the meaning of a political faction.

40 Access to the consulship was established by the Licinio-Sextian laws of 367 BCE. Livy 6.5.5; Develin 2005: 293.

41 Hölkeskamp 1993; North 2006: 260.

42 Romans also voted in an assembly called the *comitia tributa* which was based on membership in a tribe [*tribus*], which indicated a geographical area, somewhat analogous to modern voting districts in the US, not a kin-based voting group. Lintott 1999: 51.

43 Making the *plebiscita* binding on the entire populace was the final step in the struggle between the patricians and plebeians known as the Conflict of the Orders. It was achieved through the lex Hortensia in 287 BCE, not long before Plautus' birth. Raaflaub 2006: 140.

44 The property classes determined what kind of military equipment each citizen was expected to possess and maintain but were not organized based on actual military units. See Lintott 1999: 56–8.

45 This is evident in the example of Catiline, who was determined to restore his family's wealth and prestige by any means necessary. Sallust *Bellum Catilinum*; Cicero *in Catilinam* 1.
46 Yakobson (1992) argues that the urban poor would have had more political influence than is usually attributed to them, based on the large sums expended by candidates in the late Republic to secure their votes, but Lintott (1999: 57 n. 77) disagrees.
47 The translation of lines 644–6 is from Gray 1897. De Melo in the Loeb edition places the question after *fieres* at the end of line 644. I agree with Gray and Lindsay in placing the punctuation at the end of 643 and reading the *ut vindex fieres* clause with the following the sentence.
48 Hölkeskamp 1993: 24.
49 Hölkeskamp 1993: 38.
50 The phrase I have translated as "forced abroad" is *exercitus fui* in Latin, a verb form that echoes the Latin word for "army," *exercitus*, thus bolstering the connection between Charmides and the typical citizen soldier.
51 Charmides insists on a dowry of 1,000 Philippic coins (1158), one third of the total treasure as described by Callicles (*ad tria milia*, 152), though he does not specify whether the money comes from the treasure or from funds obtained abroad.

4 Religion in *Trinummus*

1 Plautinopolis is a term coined by Gratwick (1982: 113) to describe the setting of Plautine comedy with its mixture of Greek and Roman cultures.
2 For the *Cistellaria* passage, see Moore 2004; Jeppesen 2020a. For the *Rudens* prologue, see Jeppesen 2013: 165–71; Jeppesen 2016: 71. For the analysis of *Poenulus* and an overall discussion of religious parody in Plautus, see Jeppesen 2020b. For religion in Roman comedy generally, see Dunsch 2009; Dunsch 2014; Gellar-Goad 2013; Gellar-Goad 2016; Hanson 1959.
3 The phrase "The Lord requireth the heart and a willing mind" (*Doctrine and Covenants* 64:34), comes from my own faith tradition, The Church of Jesus Christ of Latter-Day Saints, but it is similar to the broken spirit and contrite heart required in Psalm 51:17 (KJV).
4 Marshall 2006: 19–20.

5 Richlin 2017: 14–15.
6 Goldberg 1998; Goldberg 2018; Marshall 2006: 40–3; Moore 1991.
7 Rehm 2007: 185.
8 Orlin 2002.
9 Schultz 2006: 124–7.
10 For verbs of petitioning in Roman prayers, see Hickson 1993: 45–50. For the adjectives *bona, fausta, felix*, see Hickson 1993: 56, 58, 63, 65. *Fortunata* seems to be a Plautine addition to more typical prayer formulae, no doubt to increase the alliteration in the line.
11 McCarthy 2000: 140.
12 For example, Trachalio in *Rudens* 702–4 prays to Venus for the safety of Palaestra and Ampelisca, but adds a slang reference to female genitalia at the end. Tranio in *Mostellaria* 528–30 finishes a prayer begun by his master Daemones by asking for a *magnum malum* for his master from Hercules. See Jeppesen 2013: 91–3, 182–3, 196–8.
13 Richlin 2017: 128–9, 247.
14 Kajava 1998: 109 describes the funeral that M. Flavius held for his mother in 328 and his subsequent election as tribune of the plebs. pp. 117–22 describe the likelihood of food, especially meat, coming from sources other than the sacrifice.
15 Scullard 1981: 186–7, 197.
16 Donahue 2003: 431–2; Scheid 2011: 268.
17 The Compitalia allows people from different classes to feast together as well, but in a domestic setting, rather than a public setting at the temple. See Scullard 1981: 58–60; Iddeng 2012: 23.
18 Scheid 2011: 268; Scullard 1981: 206.
19 Scullard 1981: 171–3.
20 Kajava 1998: 113–14.
21 Donahue, drawing on the typologies of Grignon, lists transgressive commensality as one potential category of public feasting, but Donahue focuses on the imperial *cenae*, rather than examining the Saturnalia or feast of Hercules. See Donahue 2003: 434–7. Both Gray and de Melo emphasize that, in Greek culture, it was customary to have only two banqueters per couch, while in Roman culture there would be three on a triclinium. Philto's description, however, does not explicitly say there are only two people on the couch, thus I do not think one needs to see this

passage as a reference to Greek, not Roman practices. See Gray 1897: 115–16; de Melo 2013: 166 n.18.

22 De Melo provides the quote but not a citation. Wagner also quotes this saying in his commentary, and he attributes it to Scaliger, but he notes that Scaliger does not include a source either. Ultimately, it seems that the reference to Scaliger comes from Gronovius' seventeenth-century commentary on Plautus (I consulted the digitized 1829 edition), in which he indicates that he found the quote in a letter from Scaliger about this passage, in which Scaliger says that Stasimus here behaves as a comic parasite, since all his attention is focused on food. Although the letter is cited, Gronovius includes no classical reference for the senatorial formula. See de Melo 2013: 166–7 n. 20; Gronovius 1829: Vol. 4:2164; Wagner 1872: 57–8. The quote was current in eighteenth- and nineteenth-century European literature, as a brief internet search will reveal, but when you search the corpus of classical Latin texts (using the Packard Humanities Institute database), no indication of the source of this quote is to be found. It seems, then, that this supposed senatorial formula is not of classical origin but was written later and attributed to the ancient Roman senate. Gray (1897) makes no mention in his commentary about the supposed senatorial quote but explains that Stasimus' saying means that, when it comes to food, the only distinction made is between the portion for the gods, offered in sacrifice, and the portion given to humans, which means that the human portion is available to everyone, regardless of class distinctions.

23 Plautus makes a similar joke at *Curculio* 280–7.
24 But compare Philto's very different sentiments at 339–40.
25 For a thorough treatment of hunger in Plautus, see Richlin 2017: 126–36.
26 "The Impact of the Coronavirus on Food Insecurity in 2020 & 2021" 2021.
27 Food and Agricultural Organization of the United Nations 2021.
28 De Melo 2013: 169 n. 22.
29 The manuscripts have *et Nerei* (and brother of Nereus) which is an incorrect genealogy. I have chosen to follow Scaliger's emendation, also followed by Wagner and Freeman and Sloman, and change this phrase to *aetherei* (brother of celestial Jupiter).
30 Especially the phrase *columem reducem faciunt*. See Fraenkel 2007: 159–72; Hickson-Hahn 2004.

31 This is an example of the rhetorical device praeteritio, in which a speaker says awful things about an opponent while claiming to pass over them.
32 I have changed the punctuation here from de Melo's text by placing the period at the end of line 830 so as to construe the phrase *hoc dis dignum est* ("this is worthy of the gods") more closely with the end of the line *semper mendicis modesti sint* ("may they always be kind to the poor"). I also removed the square brackets from around the second half of the line because I see no reason to remove it from the text.
33 Gellius 3.3.15; Cicero *In Verrem* 1.10.29. Conte notes that the story is "of contested authenticity" (1999: 44).
34 Gray 1897: 155; Wagner 1872: 89.
35 Carandini 2017: Vol. I 496, 499, 503, and Vol. II Tab. 208 for a map of the area.
36 Coarelli 2007: 266–7.
37 Crawford 1974: Vol. I 444–5; Vol. II LI 420/1a.

5 A Moral Play or a Play on Morals?

1 This quote has been variously attributed to Johnny Carson, Steve Martin, and Jack Handey, though I have been unable to find any specific bibliographic detail for any of these attributions.
2 By my calculation 356 out of 1,189 lines can be classified as moralizing, 29.9 percent of the total. See Appendix C for more information.
3 "The Westminster Play" 1897. For an analysis of the revised version of *Eunuchus*, see Brown 2008.
4 This performance history was compiled using the Archive of Performances of Greek and Roman Drama at Oxford. Special thanks to Fiona Macintosh and Claire Barnes for hosting me at the archive and for their guidance and advice in my research.
5 Tuohy 2002: 261 n. 159; Sanesi 1911: 143; Reinhardstöttner 1886: 37; Smith 1987: 138; *Trinummus* (1525), accessed at http://www.apgrd.ox.ac.uk/productions/production/7998 <7 May 2022>.
6 Productions at Radley College took place in 1884, 1888, and 1892. Email from Clare Sargent to Peter Brown, accessed at http://www.apgrd.ox.ac.uk/productions/sources/10128 <7 May 2022>.

7 Hains 1910.
8 "Plays for the Connoisseur" 1958; *Trinummus* (2000), accessed at http://www.apgrd.ox.ac.uk/productions/production/10447 <7 May 2022>; https://www.locridecultura.it/evento/locri-il-ctm-mette-in-scena-la-trinummus-di-plauto/ <16 May 2022>.
9 Special thanks to Elizabeth Wells and the staff at Westminster School for hosting my research trip to their archive and for their insight into the history of the school and the annual performances. All news clippings and play programmes cited below were consulted in the Westminster School Archive collection.
10 This section of the school charter is cited in Motter 1968: 86.
11 Motter 1968: 92.
12 Motter 1968: 95–6. Some exceptions to this rotation were made, such as bringing back *Amphitruo* in 1729 and 1792, and introducing *Rudens* in 1798. See Mure, Bull, and Scott 1867: Vol. 2: preface.
13 Mure, Bull, and Scott 1867: Vol. 2: xvi–xviii.
14 Epilogues were written by the headmasters, second masters, under masters, or sometimes the ushers. Richard Busby was headmaster of the school for an impressive span from 1638 to 1695 and was himself a former pupil of St. Peter's who, after success in the annual play, planned on pursuing a career in acting before being offered the headmastership. Motter 1968: 95, 102. For the plots referenced here, see "The Westminster Play" 1869; Davies 1874; "The Westminster Play" 1893; "The Westminster Play" 1897; "The Westminster Play" 1860; "Plot of the Epilogue" *Trinummus* Programme, 1879.
15 Brown 2008: 25.
16 For a discussion of the ethics of performing *Eunuchus* today, see Slater 1999.
17 Brown 20.
18 "The Westminster Play" *Daily Telegraph*, 1860.
19 "The Westminster Play" 1869.
20 Anderson 1979: 339.
21 "The Westminster Play" 1860.
22 "The Westminster Play" 1869.
23 "The Westminster Play" 1883.
24 Davies 1874.
25 "The Westminster Play" 1897.

26 Brown 2008: 23 notes that all the plays in the cycle were cut by roughly one quarter during the 1890s, for length, not for content, so that there would be more time for hobnobbing among the Old Westminsters in the intervals between acts. For the abridged script, see Plautus 1893.
27 "The Westminster Play" 1897.
28 *Famulus* was based on an edited version of the play composed by Cardinal Newman titled *Pincerna* and performed five times at the Oratory School, Edgbaston, around the same time *Trinummus* was being performed at Westminster. Brown 2008: 18 n. 6.
29 This new compromise between the Westminster traditionalists and the moral reformers managed to hold the stage until it was replaced by Plautus' *Rudens* in 1926. Brown 2008: 18.
30 "The Westminster Play" 1869.
31 *mi placet ars belli—sed non plebs squalida Nili* (note the internal rhyme in the Latin). Mure, Bull, and Scott 1906: Vol. 3:112.
32 Mure, Bull, and Scott 1906: Vol. 3:178
33 Mure, Bull, and Scott 1906: Vol. 3:179.
34 "By Pollux, this guy is certainly a specimen of the mushroom variety—his head covers himself entirely!" (*Pol hic quidem fungino genere est: captie se totum tegit*, 851).
35 Moore 1998a: 24–34.
36 This and the following quotes in this paragraph are from Mure, Bull, and Scott 1906: Vol. 3:180.
37 See the section on Poverty and Inequality in the document titled "Our Demands" on the Poor People's Campaign website, accessed at https://www.poorpeoplescampaign.org/about/our-demands/ <25 May 2022>.
38 Mure, Bull, and Scott 1906: Vol. 3:181. This line is also a humorous allusion to Vergil's famous line about Dido: "A woman was the leader of the deed" [*dux femina facti, Aeneid* 1.364].
39 Hutcheon and O'Flynn 2013: 141–68.
40 Field 1987. Line 831, *semper mendicis modesti sint*, was among the lines cut from the Westminster performance script. See Appendix B for discussion of this line from Charmides' prayer.
41 Quoted in Lefèvre 1993: 177. For more on Lessing's view of the play, see Pinna 2016.
42 Segal 1974.

43 Most notably Frank 1932. Lefèvre 1993: 177–81 includes an excellent lit review on the question of morality in *Trinummus*.
44 Lefèvre 1993.
45 Moore 1998a: 67–90, esp. 89.
46 Moore 1998a: 82.
47 For the importance of trust [*fides*] and friendship [*amicitia*] in the play, see Segal 1974; Burton 2004; Raccanelli 2016.
48 Special thanks to the students in my seminar on *Trinummus* at BYU in Fall 2021 for the suggestion.
49 Lefèvre 1993: 187.
50 Segal 1974 compares and contrasts *Trinummus* with *Mostellaria*; both plays were adapted from originals by Philemon.
51 For more on the music in *Trinummus*, see Appendix A.
52 For the distinction between marked and unmarked sententiae, see Dinter 2016: 136.
53 For sententiae in ancient comedy generally, see Dinter 2016.
54 Papaioannou 2016: 171.
55 Lefèvre 1993: 186; Segal 1974: 257.
56 "The Westminster Play" 1897; Moore 1998a: 85.
57 Alison Sharrock 2009: 175–8 calls this tactic the comic echo.
58 Moore 1998a: 89.
59 Segal 1974: 259, esp. n. 17.
60 Gratwick 1981: 334.
61 There are many textual variants and emendations for these names. De Melo 2013: 226 and Gratwick 1981:331 provide good textual notes. The text I have chosen here is de Melo's, except I have kept Leo's *Circonychus* (the *y* is short) where de Melo prints Circonīcus. This change required retaining the *fuit*, which is present in the primary manuscripts, for the sake of the meter (trochaic septenarii).
62 In poems 2 and 3 Catullus speaks of his mistress' pet sparrow [*passer*] which she enjoys playing with. This has occasionally been taken as an obscene metaphor describing how Catullus' mistress treats his penis as her pet, though not without considerable disagreement among scholars. At any rate, the Greek word for sparrow [*strouthos*] does have sexual connotations. See Green 2021; Jones 1998.
63 Leo and Gratwick are certainly correct in arguing that the name should begin with *Circo-* not *Cerco-*, since it is unlikely that Plautus would have

used the same prefix twice in his list (cf. *Cercobulus*). However, since the audience experienced this as performance not as text, the phonic similarities between the two prefixes allow for slippage between bird imagery and phallic imagery, in a way that "hawk" and "penis" do not permit in English. I chose "cock" as a translation that allows the same type of double meaning—besides Nighthawk and Nightcock sound almost identical in English.

64 De Melo 2013: 227 suggests the connection between the name Cliff and the idea of danger. Gratwick prints Crimnus, which he says is a made-up name that sounds like the Latin word for "crime," *crimen*.

65 De Melo 2013: 227 says that *collops* can mean "hermaphrodite," but the comic fragments cited in LSJ (Eubolus 11, Diphilus 43.22) seem to pair this word with prostitution as well.

66 See *Trinummus* 1016, where Charmides says, "Curculio must be this guy's trainer!" (Gratwick: *Curculiost exercitor*; de Melo: *Gurgulio est exercitor*— his gullet is his trainer). See Gratwick 1981: 335–41; Slater 1987.

67 Welsh 2006; Fontaine 2010: 228–30.

68 Moore 1998a: 88.

69 "The Westminster Play" 1897.

Appendix B: A Textual Note on Line 831

1 De Melo, Ernout, Freeman and Sloman, Gray, Langen, Leo, and Mueller all favor deleting the line while Lindsay, Niemeyer, and Wagner accept the text as is, with Niemeyer and Wagner both adding additional half-lines that emphasize Neptune's fair treatment of the poor. Wagner follows Hermann in moving the phrase *et nobilest apud homines* ["and is well known among people"] from the end of line 828 to the end of line 831 and rendering it *secus nobilis apud homines* ["differently among the nobility"]. Niemeyer conjectures that the phrase *Potentes perpetuo perdant* ["May they destroy the powerful"] could be added to complete the line and give it eight anapests to match the preceding lines. It is not uncommon, however, to have a few half-lines in anapestic passages. Niemeyer suggests that Charmides presents the audience with a view of the gods that would accord with their views. De Melo 2013; Ernout 2003; Freeman and Sloman 1883; Gray 1897; Langen 1880: 277–84; Leo 1896; Lindsay 1905; Niemeyer 1925; Wagner 1872.

2 *Pace* Freeman and Sloman 1883: 101 who refer to line 831 is a "mutilated fragment of a line that gives no good sense."
3 Pal. Lat. 1615, 198r. https://digi.vatlib.it/view/MSS_Pal.lat.1615.
4 The normally long syllable -*est*- in *modesti* must scan as short: *mŏdĕstī sīnt*. However, this same situation occurs at *Miles* 69 with the word *mŏlĕstae*. Furthermore, it is common for cretic rhythms (long–short–long) to scan as dactyls in anapestic meter, so here the long syllable at the end of *mendicis* combines with the first two syllables of *modesti* to form a dactyl. Additionally, it is not uncommon in Plautus for the letter *s* not to make position when paired with another consonant, though this usually happens when *s* is at the end of a word. Lindsay 1905: loc. cit.; Moore 2012b: 230; Niemeyer 1925: 112; Willcock 1991: 143–5.
5 Leo 1896 Vol. 2:442.
6 Gray 1897: 155.

Bibliography

Adler, E. 2016. *Classics, the Culture Wars, and Beyond.* Ann Arbor: University of Michigan Press.

Anderson, W. S. 1979. "Plautus' 'Trinummus': The Absurdity of Officious Morality." *Traditio* 35: 333–45.

Anderson, W. S. 1993. *Barbarian Play: Plautus' Roman Comedy.* Toronto: University of Toronto Press.

Batstone, W. 2006. "Literature." In Rosenstein, N., and Morstein-Marx, R., eds. *A Companion to the Roman Republic.* Malden, MA: Blackwell. 543–63.

Beard, M., North, J., and Price, S. 1998. *Religions of Rome: Volume 2: A Sourcebook.* Cambridge: Cambridge University Press.

Beare, W. 1933. "Two Books on Plautus." Edited by Günther Jachmann and Carrie May Kurrelmeyer. *Classical Review* 47 (4): 140–1.

Bernstein, F. 2007. "Complex Rituals: Games and Processions in Republican Rome." In Rüpke, J., ed. *A Companion to Roman Religion.* Malden, MA: Blackwell. 222–34.

Brown, P. G. McC. 2002. "Actors and Actor-Managers at Rome in the Time of Plautus and Terence." In Easterling, P., and Hall, E., eds. *Greek and Roman Actors: Aspects of an Ancient Profession.* Cambridge: Cambridge University Press. 225–37.

Brown, P. G. McC. 2008. "The Eunuch Castrated: Bowdlerization in the Text of the Westminster Latin Play." *International Journal of the Classical Tradition* 15 (1): 16–28.

Brunt, P. A. 1982. "Nobilitas and Novitas." *Journal of Roman Studies* 72: 1–17.

Burton, P. J. 2004. "*Amicitia* in Plautus: A Study of Roman Friendship Processes." *American Journal of Philology* 125 (2): 209–43.

Coarelli, F. 2007. *Rome and Environs: An Archaeological Guide.* Berkeley: University of California Press.

Conte, G. B. 1999. *Latin Literature: A History.* Translated by Joseph B. Solodow. Baltimore: Johns Hopkins University Press.

Crawford, M. H. 1974. *Roman Republican Coinage.* Cambridge: Cambridge University Press.

Csapo, E. 2005. *Theories of Mythology.* Malden, MA: Blackwell.

Damen, M. 1989. "Actors and Act-Divisions in the Greek Original of Plautus' 'Menaechmi.'" *Classical World* 82 (6): 409–20.

Damen, M. 1992. "Translating Scenes: Plautus' Adaptation of Menander's 'Dis Exapaton.'" *Phoenix* 46 (3): 205–31.

Davies, M. 1874. "The Westminster Play." *The Pictorial Times*, December 26.

Develin, R. 2005. "The Integration of the Plebeians into the Political Order after 366 B.C." In Raaflaub, K. A., ed. *Social Struggle in Archaic Rome: New Perspectives on the Conflict of the Orders. Expanded and Updated Edition.* Malden, MA: Blackwell. 293–311.

Dinter, M. T. 2016. "Sententiousness in Roman Comedy-A Moralizing Reading." In Frangoulidis, S., Harrison, S. J., and Manuwald, G., eds. *Roman Drama and its Contexts.* Trends in Classics. Berlin: De Gruyter. 34: 127–41.

Donahue, J. F. 2003. "Toward a Typology of Roman Public Feasting." *American Journal of Philology* 124 (3): 423–41.

Duckworth, G. E. 1994 (1952). *The Nature of Roman Comedy: A Study in Popular Entertainment.* 2nd ed. Norman, OK: University of Oklahoma Press.

Dunsch, B. 2009. "Religion in der Römischen Komödie: Einige programmatische Überlegungen." In *Römische Religion im Historische Wandel.* Stuttgart: Steiner. 17–56.

Dunsch, B. 2014. "Religion in Roman Comedy." In Fontaine, M., and Scafuro, A. C., eds. *Oxford Handbook of Greek and Roman Comedy.* Oxford: Oxford University Press. 634–54.

Ernout, A. 2003. *Plaute: Comédies Tome VII—Trinummus, Truculentus, Vidularia, Fragments.* Paris: Les Belles Lettres.

Ferrary, J.-L. 2006. "Philhellenism." Edited by Hubert Cancik, Helmuth Schneider, Christine F. Salazar, Manfred Landfester, and Francis G. Gentry. *Brills New Pauly.* Leiden: Brill.

Field, J. 1987. *The King's Nurseries: The Story of Westminster School.* London: James & James.

Fontaine, M. 2010. *Funny Words in Plautine Comedy.* Oxford: Oxford University Press.

Food and Agricultural Organization of the United Nations. 2021. "Europe and Central Asia—Regional Overview of Food Security and Nutrition 2021: Statistics and Trends." Budapest.

Fraenkel, E. 1922. *Plautinisches im Plautus.* Berlin: Weidmann.

Fraenkel, E. 2007. *Plautine Elements in Plautus: (Plautinisches im Plautus).* Trans. F. Muecke. Oxford: Oxford University Press.

Frank, T. 1932. "Some Political Allusions in Plautus' Trinummus." *American Journal of Philology* 53 (2): 152–6.

Freeman, C. E., and Sloman, A., eds. 1883. *T. Macci Plauti Trinummus.* Oxford: Clarendon Press.

Gabba, E. 1989. "Rome and Italy in the Second Century B.C." In Astin, A. E., Walbank, F. W., Frederiksen, M. W., and Ogilvie, R. M., eds. *The Cambridge Ancient History Vol. VII: Rome and the Mediterranean to 133 B.C.*, 2nd ed. Cambridge: Cambridge University Press. 197–243.

Gellar-Goad, T. H. M. 2013. "Religious Ritual and Family Dynamics in Terence." *A Companion to Terence.* Malden, MA: Wiley-Blackwell. 156–74.

Gellar-Goad, T. H. M. 2016. "Plautus' *Curculio* and the Case of the Pious Pimp." In Frangoulidis, S., Harrison, S. J., and Manuwald, G., eds. *Roman Drama and its Contexts.* Trends in Classics. Berlin: De Gruyter. 231–52.

Goldberg, S. M. 1990. "Act to Action in Plautus' 'Bacchides.'" *Classical Philology* 85 (3): 191–201.

Goldberg, S. M. 1998. "Plautus on the Palatine." *Journal of Roman Studies* 88: 1–20.

Goldberg, S. M. 2018. "Theater without Theaters: Seeing Plays the Roman Way." *TAPA* 148 (1): 139–72.

Gratwick, A. S. 1981. "Curculio's Last Bow: Plautus, 'Trinummus' IV. 3." *Mnemosyne* 34 (3/4): 331–50.

Gratwick, A. S. 1982. "Drama: Light Drama." In Kenney, E. J., ed. *Cambridge History of Classica Literature.* Cambridge University Press. 77–137.

Gray, J. H., ed. 1897. *T. Macci Plauti Trinummus.* Cambridge: Cambridge University Press.

Green, A. 2021. "Lesbia's Controversial Bird: Testing the Cases for and against Passer as Sparrow." *Antichthon* 55: 6–20.

Gronovius, J. F., ed. 1829. *M. Accii Plauti Comœdiæ.* Vol. 4. London: A. J. Valpy.

Gruen, E. S. 1996. *Studies in Greek Culture and Roman Policy.* Berkeley: University of California Press.

Gruen, E. S. 2014. "Roman Comedy and the Social Scene." In Fontaine, M., and Scafuro, A. C., eds. *Oxford Handbook of Greek and Roman Comedy.* Oxford: Oxford University Press. 601–14.

Hains, D. D. 1910. "Greek Plays in America." *Classical Journal* 6 (1): 24–39.

Handley, E. W. 1968. *Menander and Plautus; A Study in Comparison.* London: H. K. Lewis.

Hanses, M. 2020. *The Life of Comedy after the Death of Plautus and Terence.* Ann Arbor: University of Michigan Press.

Hanson, J. A. 1959. "Plautus as a Source Book for Roman Religion." *TAPA* 90: 48–101.

Hickson, F. 1993. *Roman Prayer Language: Livy and the Aneid [Sic] of Vergil.* Leipzig: Teubner.

Hickson-Hahn, F. 2004. "The Politics of Thanksgiving." In Konrad, C. F., ed. *Augusto Augurio Rerum Humanarum Divinarum Commentationes in Honorem Jerzy Linderski.* Stuttgart: Steiner. 31–51.

Hölkeskamp, K. J. 1993. "Conquest, Competition and Consensus: Roman Expansion in Italy and the Rise of the 'Nobilitas.'" *Historia: Zeitschrift für Alte Geschichte* 42 (1): 12–39.

Hutcheon, L., and O'Flynn, S. 2013. *A Theory of Adaptation.* London: Routledge.

Iddeng, J. W. 2012. "What is a Graeco-Roman Festival? A Polythetic Approach." In Brandt, J. R., and Iddeng, J. W., eds. *Greek and Roman Festivals: Content, Meaning, and Practice.* Oxford: Oxford University Press. 11–38.

Jeppesen, S. A. 2013. "Performing Religious Parody in Plautine Comedy." Dissertation, University of California, Santa Barbara.

Jeppesen, S. A. 2016. "Dictating Parody in Plautus' *Rudens*." *Didaskalia* 12: 69–92.

Jeppesen, S. A. 2020a. "Meaningful Mispronunciations: Religious Parody in Plautus' *Cistellaria* 512–27." In Demetriou, C., and Papaioannou, S., eds. *Plautus Doctus: New Insights into Cultural and Literary Aspects of Plautine Comedy.* Pierides. Newcastle upon Tyne: Cambridge Scholars Publishing.

Jeppesen, S. A. 2020b. "Religion in and around Plautus." In Dutsch, D., and Franko, G. F., eds. *A Companion to Plautus.* Hoboken, NJ: Wiley-Blackwell. 317–30.

Jones, J. W. 1998. "Catullus' 'Passer' as 'Passer.'" *Greece Rome* 45 (2): 188–94.

Kajava, M. 1998. "Visceratio." *Arctos* 32: 109–31.

Langen, P. 1880. *Beiträge zur Kritik und Erklärung des Plautus.* Leipzig: Teubner.

Lefèvre, E. 1993. "Politics and Society in Plautus' 'Trinummus.'" In Scodel, R., ed. *Theater and Society in the Classical World.* Ann Arbor: University of Michigan Press. 177–90.

Leigh, M. 2004. *Comedy and the Rise of Rome.* Oxford: Oxford University Press.

Leo, F. 1895. *Plautinische Forschungen zur Kritik und Geschichte der Komödie.* Berlin: Weidmann.

Leo, F., ed. 1896. *Plavti Comoediae.* Vol. 2. Berlin: Weidmann.

Lindsay, W. M., ed. 1905. *Plautus: Comoediae, Vol. II.* Oxford: Oxford University Press.

Lintott, A. 1999. *The Constitution of the Roman Republic.* Oxford: Oxford University Press.

Manuwald, G. 2011. *Roman Republican Theatre*. Cambridge: Cambridge University Press.

Marshall, C. W. 2006. *The Stagecraft and Performance of Roman Comedy*. Cambridge: Cambridge University Press.

Marshall, C. W. 2008. "Plautinisches im Plautus." by E. Fraenkel, Tomas Drevikovsky, and Frances Muecke. *Classical Review* 58 (1): 110–12.

McCarthy, K. 2000. *Slaves, Masters, and the Art of Authority in Plautine Comedy*. Princeton: Princeton University Press.

de Melo, W., ed. 2013. *Plautus: Stichus; Three-Dollar Day; Truculentus; The Tale of a Traveling-Bag; Fragments*. Cambridge, MA: Harvard University Press.

Miller, N., trans. 1987. *Menander: Plays and Fragments*. London: Penguin Books.

Moore, T. J. 1991. "Palliata Togata: Plautus, Curculio 462–86." *American Journal of Philology* 112 (3): 343–62.

Moore, T. J. 1998a. *The Theater of Plautus: Playing to the Audience*. Austin: University of Texas Press.

Moore, T. J. 1998b. "Music and Structure in Roman Comedy." *American Journal of Philology* 119 (2): 245–73.

Moore, T. J. 2004. "Confusing the Gods: Plautus, *Cistellaria* 512–527." *Augusto Augurio Rerum Humanarum Divinarum Commentationes in Honorem Jerzy Linderski*. Stuttgart: Steiner. 53–67.

Moore, T. J. 2012a. *Music in Roman Comedy*. Cambridge: Cambridge University Press.

Moore, T. J. 2012b. "Don't Skip the Meter! Introducing Students to the Music of Roman Comedy." *Classical Journal* 108 (2): 218–34.

Motter, T. H. V. 1968. *The School Drama in England*. Port Washington, NY: Kennikat Press.

Muecke, F. 1985. "Names and Players: The Sycophant Scene of the 'Trinummus' (Trin. 4.2)." *TAPA* 115: 167–86.

Muecke, F. 1986. "Plautus and the Theater of Disguise." *Classical Antiquity* 5 (2): 216–29.

Mure, J., Bull, H., and Scott, C. B., eds. 1867. *Lusus Alteri Westmonasterienses sive Prologi et Epilogi: Ad Fabulas in Sancti Petri Collegio Actas*. Vol. 2. London: J. H. et J. Parker.

Mure, J., Bull, H., and Scott, C. B., eds. 1906. *Lusus Alteri Westmonasterienses sive Prologi et Epilogi: Ad Fabulas in Sancti Petri Collegio Actas*. Vol. 3. London: J. H. et J. Parker.

Niemeyer, M., ed. 1925. *Ausgewählte Komödien des T. Maccius Plautus: Trinummus*. Leipzig: Teubner.

North, J. A. 2006. "The Constitution of the Roman Republic." In Morstein-Marx, R., and Rosenstein, N., eds. *A Companion to the Roman Republic*. Malden, MA: Blackwell. 256–77.

Norwood, G. 1923. *The Art of Terence*. Oxford: Blackwell.

O'Bryhim, S. 2020. "Stock Characters and Stereotypes." In Dutsch, D., and Franko, G. F., eds. *A Companion to Plautus*. Hoboken, NJ: Wiley-Blackwell. 123–34.

Orlin, E. 2002. *Temples, Religion, and Politics in the Roman Republic*. Leiden: Brill.

Owens, W. M. 1994. "The Third Deception in *Bacchides*: Fides and Plautus' Originality." *American Journal of Philology* 115 (3): 381–407.

Papaioannou, S. 2016. "Plautus Undoing Himself—What Is Funny and What Is Plautine in *Stichus* and *Trinummus*." In Frangoulidis, S., Harrison, S. J., and Manuwald, G., eds. *Roman Drama Its Contexts*. Trends in Classics. Berlin: De Gruyter. 34: 167–201.

Petrone, G. 2016. "Un Intrigo a fin di Bene: Esemplarità del *Trinummus*." In *Lecturae Plautinae Sarsinates XIX Trinummus*. Urbino: QuattroVenti.

Pfeiffer, R. 1976. *History of Classical Scholarship from 1300 to 1850*. Oxford: Oxford University Press.

Pinna, G. 2016. "Peripezie dell' Amicizia: Lessing e Il *Trinummus*." In Raffaelli, R., and Tontini, A., eds. *Lecturae Plautinae Sarsinates XIX Trinummus*. Urbino: QuattroVenti. 83–99.

Plautus, T. M. 1893. *The Trinummus of Plautus: As It Is Performed at the Royal College of St. Peter, Westminster*. Translated by Bonnell Thornton. Westminster: Ashburn House.

"Plays for the Connoisseur." 1958. *The Times*, December 11.

Raaflaub, K. A. 2006. "Between Myth and History: Rome's Rise from Village to Empire (The Eighth Century to 264)." In Morstein-Marx, R., and Rosenstein, N., eds. *A Companion to the Roman Republic*. Malden, MA: Blackwell. 125–46.

Raccanelli, R. 2016. "Reti di *Amicitia* nel *Trinummus*: Paradossi delle Relazioni e Paradossi Comici." In Raffaelli, R., and Tontini, A., eds. *Lecturae Plautinae Sarsinates XIX Trinummus*. Urbino: QuattroVenti.

Rehm, R. 2007. "Festivals and Audiences in Athens and Rome." In McDonald, M., and Walton, J. M., eds. *Cambridge Companion to Greek and Roman Theatre*. Cambridge: Cambridge University Press. 184–201.

von Reinhardstöttner, K. 1886. *Plautus: Spätere Bearbeitungen plautinischer Lustspiele*. Leipzig: W. Friedrich.

Richlin, A. 2017. *Slave Theater in the Roman Republic: Plautus and Popular Comedy*. Cambridge: Cambridge University Press.

Rosenmeyer, P. A. 1995. "Enacting the Law: Plautus' Use of the Divorce Formula on Stage." *Phoenix* 49 (3): 201–17.

Sanesi, I. 1911. *La Commedia*. Milan: Vallardi.

Scheid, J. 2011. "Sacrifices for Gods and Ancestors." In Rüpke, J., ed. *A Companion to Roman Religion*. Malden, MA: Wiley-Blackwell. 263–71.

Schultz, C. E. 2006. *Women's Religious Activity in the Roman Republic*. Chapel Hill: The University of North Carolina Press.

Scott, J. C. 2008. *Domination and the Arts of Resistance: Hidden Transcripts*. New Haven: Yale University Press.

Scullard, H. H. 1981. *Festivals and Ceremonies of the Roman Republic*. Ithaca, NY: Cornell University Press.

Segal, E. 1968. *Roman Laughter: The Comedy of Plautus*. Cambridge, MA: Harvard University Press.

Segal, E. 1974. "The Purpose of the *Trinummus*: For J. Arthur Hanson." *American Journal of Philology* 95 (3): 252–64.

Sharrock, A. 2014. "Reading Plautus' *Trinummus*: Who'd Bother?" In *Plautine Trends: Studies in Plautine Comedy and its Reception*. Berlin: De Gruyter. 167–96.

Sharrock, A. 2009. *Reading Roman Comedy: Poetics and Playfulness in Plautus and Terence*. Cambridge: Cambridge University Press.

Shelton, J.-A. 1998. *As the Romans Did: A Sourcebook in Roman Social History*. Oxford: Oxford University Press.

Slater, N. W. 1985. *Plautus in Performance: The Theatre of the Mind*. Princeton: Princeton University Press.

Slater, N. W. 1987. "The Dates of Plautus' *Curculio* and *Trinummus* Reconsidered." *American Journal of Philology* 108 (2): 264–9.

Slater, N. W. 1999. "*Humani Nil a Me Alienum Puto*: The Ethics of Terentian Performance." *Syllecta Classica* 10: 1–21.

Smith, B. R. 1987. *Ancient Scripts and Modern Experience on the English Stage, 1500–1700*. Princeton: Princeton University Press.

"The Impact of the Coronavirus on Food Insecurity in 2020 & 2021." 2021. Feeding America.

"The Westminster Play." 1860. *The Daily Telegraph*, December 19.

"The Westminster Play." 1869. *The Graphic*, December 25.

"The Westminster Play." 1883. *The Saturday Review*, December 22.

"The Westminster Play." 1893. *The Graphic*, December 23.

"The Westminster Play." 1897. *The Standard*, December 17.
Tuohy, T. 2002. *Herculean Ferrara: Ercole D'Este (1471–1505) and the Invention of a Ducal Capital*. Cambridge: Cambridge University Press.
Tyson, L. 2014. *Critical Theory Today: A User-Friendly Guide*. 3rd ed. London: Routledge.
Wagner, W., ed. 1872. *T. Macci Plauti Trinummus with Notes Critical and Exegetical*. Cambridge: Deighton Bell and Company.
Welsh, J. T. 2006. "Cato, Plautus, and the Metaphorical Use of Anulus." *Phoenix* 60 (1/2): 133–9.
Willcock, M. M. 1991. *Plautus: Pseudolus*. London: Bristol Classical Press.
Witzke, S. S. 2015. "Harlots, Tarts, and Hussies?: A Problem of Terminology for Sex Labor in Roman Comedy." *Helios* 42 (1): 7–27.
Yakobson, A. 1992. "*Petitio et Largitio*: Popular Participation in the Centuriate Assembly of the Late Republic." *Journal of Roman Studies* 82: 32–52.
Zagagi, N. 1980. *Tradition and Originality in Plautus: Studies of the Amatory Motifs in Plautine Comedy*. Göttingen: Vandenhoeck & Ruprecht.

Index

Note: References followed by "n" refer to notes.

adaptation(s)
    Greek originals 53–62
    Hutcheon's theory 59, 115
    transculturation 115
Adelphi (Terence) 102
aemulatio 59
alliteration 85
Altertumswissenschaft (Science of Antiquity) 55, 56, 108
Amphitruo (Plautus) 39, 102, 145n18, 154n12
Anderson, William S. 37, 58, 105, 149n36
Andria (Terence) 102
Andronicus, Livius 7, 60
Antiochus III 14, 66, 74
Appian 63
architecti doli 10, 41, 48; see also trickster
Aristophanes of Byzantium 56
Asinaria (Plautus) 30
Astaire, Fred 119
Athens, actors in 5
Aulularia (Plautus) 58

Bacchides (Plautus) 53
Barnes, Claire 153n4
Beare, W. 57–8
Book of Mormon: The Musical 79
Brown, P. G. 155n26
Buckland, Dean 105

Caecilius 61, 148n24
Callicles (character) 1, 9, 23, 26, 30–3, 36, 37, 41–4, 48, 49, 61, 65–6, 68, 73, 111–13
    dictating prayer 84–6, 92
    Megaronides' speeches 1 17–19
Cappadox (character) 127–8
Captivi (Plautus) 22
Cato the Elder 116, 117
    as censor 118, 119
Catullus
    mistress 156n62
Ceres 81, 96
Cerialia 81–2
Charmides (character) 1, 9, 11–12, 14, 23, 28, 30, 32, 40–52, 104, 108, 112, 118, 123, 124
    absence of 65–7
    house/household 9, 61, 74–6, 94, 129
    moral maxims 125–6
    prayer to Neptune 92–6
charming old man (character) 23–4
Christianity 80
Cicero 5, 61–2, 73
Circus Flaminius 82, 95–6
Cistellaria (Plautus) 5, 149n37
class inequality. *See* social class(es)
clever slave (character) 20, 22–3, 25–6, 30, 31, 32–3, 38, 39, 46, 50, 52, 57
comedy, Roman 3–4, 17, 53–62
    characters and plots 10–11, 20
    criticism 21
    love plot 26–7
    methods/techniques 13–14
    palliatae 7, 8, 11, 15–16, 59
    religion in 79–96

conman (character) 9, 24, 28, 30, 33, 42, 43–9, 51, 52, 61, 96–7, 103–4, 108, 114, 123, 146n33
cultic prayer 85–6, 92
Curculio (Plautus) 6, 127

Davies, Maurice 107
de Melo, Wolfgang 14, 47, 88, 126, 145n13, 150n47, 151–2nn21–22, 153n32, 156n61, 157nn64–5
Dis Exapaton (Menander) 53
dowry 9, 12, 20, 35, 36, 37–9, 41–2, 44, 48, 68, 71, 73–4, 76, 91, 108, 122, 123, 124, 150n1; *see also* marriage
Duckworth, G. E. 56–7
dutiful slave (character) 24

epulum Iovis. *See* feast of Jupiter (*epulum Iovis*)
Eunuchus (Terence) 100, 102, 104–7, 109

Famulus (*Footman*) 109, 155n28
farm 9, 11, 12, 38, 39, 40, 63, 65, 66–7, 73–6
  prodigies 91–2
feasts/feasting 86–90
  class segregation and discourse 87–90
  feast of Hercules 87
  funerals 87
  public 86–7
  Saturnalia 87
female character 27, 68, 109–10, 144n7
festivals, Roman 1–4, 81–4
Forum 82
Fraenkel, Eduard 11, 56, 57
funerals 87

games for the Great Mother Goddess 2–3, 14, 47, 81, 82, 83

Games of Apollo (*ludi Apollinares*) 2, 81, 82, 95
Garner, Eric 16
gender roles 109–10; *see also* female character
German classicism 54–5
go (*abi*) 95
Gracchus, Tiberius 63–4
Graphic 106
Gratwick, A. S. 126–7, 150n1, 156–7n63, 156n61, 157n64
Gray, J. H. 95, 136, 145n17, 148n29, 150n47, 151n21, 152n22
Greek New Comedy 25, 53, 56
Greek plays 53–62

Handley, E. W. 53
Hannibal 6–7, 15, 62
The Haunted House. *See Mostellaria* (Plautus)
Heautontimoroumenos (Terence) 102
Heyne, Christian Gottlob 54
Hippocrates 127
Holkeskamp, K. J. 72
Homeric Question 55
honos 71–2
hunger 89–90
Hutcheon, Linda 11, 59, 115
Hypsaeus, P. Plautius 96

Iliad (Homer) 55
infamia 5, 143n4
Inopia 51, 64, 76, 113, 114

Jachmann, Gunther 56, 57
Jones, Sir William 147n6

Kramden, Ralph 19

land grants 62
land reforms 63–4
Latin plays, Westminster School 101–2, 105
Lefevre, E. 116, 118–19

Leo, Friedrich 56, 57, 135, 136, 143n5, 147n11, 149n36, 156n63
Lesbonicus (character) 9, 11–12, 20, 23, 27, 30, 36–42, 46, 49–50, 65–7, 86–87, 91, 94, 108, 111–15, 118, 123, 130
   as blocking character 10, 38
   expenditures or spending habits 68
   family background and social class 69–73
   farm 73–6
   wealthy friends 67–73
Lessing 116
Life of Brian (Monty Python) 79
Livius Andronicus 7
ludi Apollinares. *See* Games of Apollo (*ludi Apollinares*)
ludi Megalenses. *See* games for the Great Mother Goddess
ludi plebeii. *See* Plebeian Games (*ludi plebeii*)
ludi Romani. *See* Roman Games (*ludi Romani*)
Luxuria 64, 67
Lysiteles (character) 9, 13, 23, 33–7, 39, 52, 58, 68, 105, 107–8, 110, 112
   Anderson's description of 105
   Lesbonicus' family 69–74
   Philto's moral speech and sententiae 119–23, 125
   song and dance about rejecting love 119

Macintosh, Fiona 153n4
Magna Mater (deity) 81, 82, 83
marriage 9, 10, 26, 28, 36–9, 41, 43, 44, 48, 69–71, 73, 76, 86, 122–3, 124; *see also* dowry
Marshall, C. W. 82
McCarthy, Kathleen 85
Megaronides (character) 1, 9, 23, 26, 30–3, 36, 41–3, 45, 48–51, 61, 65, 66, 108, 112–13
   moralizing speech 117–19, 122, 124
Menander 7, 22, 37, 53, 56, 58, 77, 121
metatheatrical humor 14
middle class, Roman 11–12, 15
   economic distress 74
Miles Gloriosus (Plautus) 101, 102, 144n8, 158n4
Molière 107
Monty Python 79
Moore, Timothy 45, 49, 123, 128, 145n14
moralizing speeches and sententiae 13, 116–28, 137–41
   hypocrisy 116, 118–19
   Megaronides' speeches 117–19
   Philto and Lysiteles dialogue 119–23
   repetition 123–4
   as satire 116, 121–3
   scholarly opinions 116
   Stasimus' speech 123–8
mores 117
Mostellaria (Plautus) 32, 37, 48, 92, 119, 129
Musgrave, Thomas 105
music/musical structure 33, 49, 119, 131–3

Neptune, prayer to 92–6
   language 92–3
   social classes 93–6
Nicene Creed 80
Niemeyer, M. 157n1
Norwood, Gilbert 58

O'Bryhim, Shawn 38
Odyssey (Homer) 55
old men (character) 9, 10, 20, 23, 25, 26, 28, 30–8, 40, 41–5, 48–52, 108, 123
ordo 93–4
Ovid 22

pallium 7
Papaionannou, Sophia 51–2, 121
patricians 69–73; *see also* plebeians
Persa (Plautus) 30
Philemon 7, 12, 37, 54, 58, 59, 77, 128, 129
philhellenism 55–60
Philto 1, 9, 13, 23, 26, 28, 34, 35, 36–40, 43, 50, 51, 68, 74, 90, 94, 108, 110, 112, 114
  civic duty 64
  class discourse 89
  feasting 86, 87
  Lesbonicus' family 69–73
  moral speech and sententiae 119–23, 124, 125
  Stasimus describing prodigies 91–2
Phormio (Terence) 102
Plautine Elements in Plautus (Fraenkel) 11
Plautinische Forschungen (Leo) 57
Plautinisches im Plautus (Fraenkel) 57
Plautinisches und Attisches (Jachmann) 57
Plautinopolis 79, 150n1
Plautus 1, 4–8, 89–90
  adaptation of Greek originals 53–62
    classicists studying 11, 56–8
  Amphitruo 39, 102, 145n18, 154n12
  Asinaria 30
  Aulularia 58
  Bacchides 53
  Captivi 22
  Cistellaria 5, 149n37
  Curculio 6, 127
  death 5, 87
  double entendre 127–8
  events inflecting work 6–7
  Greek words usage 126
  Miles Gloriosus 101, 102, 144n8, 158n4

Mostellaria 32, 37, 48, 92, 119, 129
Persa 30
Poenulus 6, 150n2
reading, reasons for 15–17
Rudens 99, 124, 147n18, 149n37, 151n12, 155n29
Trinummus (*see Trinummus*)
Plebeian Games (*ludi plebeii*) 2, 81, 82, 86, 90, 95, 96
plebeians 69–73; *see also* patricians
Pliny 85
Poenulus (Plautus) 6, 150n2
prayer(s) 80
  alliteration 85
  cultic 85–6, 92
  language 85, 92
  to Neptune 92–6
  public 85
  synonyms 85
  thanksgiving 93
prodigies 90–2
  description 91
  expiatory actions/sacrifices 91
  senate collecting reports 91
Prolegomena ad Homerum (Wolf) 55
prologues 102–3
Proto-Indo-European language 147n6
Pseudolus (Plautus) 46
pseudoreligious performances 12
public land (*ager publicus*) 62–3

Quellenforschung 55, 56, 57

Rehm, Rush 83
religion, Roman 79–96
  festivals 1–4, 81–4
  important aspects 80–4
  orthodoxy *vs.* orthopraxy 80–1
  polytheism 83–4
  public affair 81–3
religious parodies 12, 79–80
  feasts/feasting 86–90

festivals 83–4
orthopraxy *vs.* orthodoxy 80–1
prayer(s) (*see* prayer(s))
prodigies 90–2
Renaissance 54
repetitions 123–4
reviews/reviewers, of Westminster
    School productions 106–9
Ribbeck 116
Richlin, Amy 15–16, 82, 95, 143n5
Roman Games (*ludi Romani*) 1–2, 7,
    81, 82, 86, 90
Rudens (Plautus) 99, 124, 147n18,
    149n37, 151n12, 155n29
Russell, John 105

sacrifices. *See* expiatory actions/
    sacrifices
Sarsina 5
Saturday Review 106–7
Saturnalia 87
Scipio Africanus 7
Scott, James C. 16
Second Punic War 6–7, 15, 61, 62, 64
Segal, Erich 8, 116, 145n11, 145n21,
    156n50
Seleucia (Hellenistic Greek city) 66
sententiae. *See* moralizing speeches
    and sententiae
Shakespeare, William 107
Sharrock, Alison 8, 20
Shelton, Jo-Ann 63
Slater, Niall 14
Slave Theater in the Roman Republic
    (Richlin) 15–16
Standard 107
Stasimus (character) 9, 11, 12, 20,
    22, 24, 30, 45, 47, 49–52, 66,
    73, 74, 100, 103, 104, 110,
    117
    class discourse 87–9
    conflicted identity 40
    deception scene 91–2
    describing prodigies 91–2
    moralizing speech 123–8

    religious discourse 90–2
    as trickster 38–41

terminus ante quem 14
terminus post quem 14
Thensauros (Philemon) 58
treasure 9, 10, 12, 14, 30–2, 41, 42, 44,
    61, 73, 76, 103, 111, 129–30,
    150n51
trickster 38–41
Trinummus (Plautus) 8–15
    actors and roles in 49–51
    as an underdog story 8
    character/character types (*see*
        individual entries)
    complaints/questions readers
        having with 10–15
    date of the play (first
        performance) 14–15
    documented performances
        101
    etymology 61
    as experimental theater 51–2
    Greek model (adaptation)
        58–62
    performance history 100–1
    plot 9–10, 20–1, 61
    prologue to 59–60
    religious parodies (*see* religious
        parodies)
    Westminster School productions
        (*see* Westminster School
        productions)
    Wilamowitz-Moellendorf on 8
trochaic septenarii 49

Varro 6
Vidularia (Plautus) 5

Wagner, W. 95, 152n22, 157n1
Wells, Elizabeth 154n9
Westminster School productions
    100–19
    economic and class concerns
        110–16

of *Eunuchus* 104–5
female character/gender roles 109–10
historical background 101–2
Latin plays 101–2, 105
reviews and reviewers 105–9

Wilamowitz-Moellendorf, Ulrich von 8
Winckelmann, Johann Joachim 54, 55
Wolf, Friedrich August 54–5

young lover (character) 23

Printed in the USA
CPSIA information can be obtained
at www.ICGtesting.com
LVHW011508061023
760361LV00005B/183